LOST AND FOUND

LOST
AND
FOUND

a prodigal's journey home

RHODA SCHULTZ

credo
house publishers

Lost and Found

Copyright © 2018 by Rhoda Schultz

All rights reserved.

Published in the United States by Credo House Publishers,
a division of Credo Communications, LLC, Grand Rapids, Michigan
credohousepublishers.com

ISBN: 978-1-625861-04-7

Cover and interior design by Sharon VanLoozenoord
Editing by Donna Huisjen

Printed in the United States of America

First edition

Contents

Foreword

"Strong and Brave." This is one of the numerous nicknames my dad used to call me. He has a gift for giving each of us kids, and now his grandkids, ridiculously good nicknames. Just when you think he's exhausted all fun twists on our names, he keeps pulling them out of his pocket. Strong and Brave. It's not even really a name, but it's what my parents would say to me every time I was within earshot.

I was tuned to their voices when I was on a playing field. Through a sea of noise, I could always hear their encouraging voices when I walked up to bat or took my helmet off. "You can do it, Brave. You got this, June." Another nickname. "June" is short for June Craiger, which is a twist on Craig Junior. The nickname "Strong and Brave" manifested a level of resiliency in me.

This story is not about me. It's not about my parents, who served me every day for a year while I was in work release. This story is not about my siblings, my grandparents, or my friends who stuck by me and encouraged me during that year. It isn't a story about "things to do" for a teenage boy to avoid drug addiction, jail, and crippling anxiety.

This story is about the finished work of Jesus on the cross.

The finished work of Jesus means that I am a new creation. It means that I am saved through grace, which enables me to be free from my sin and walk in sonship. Romans 8:17 identifies me as a co-heir with Christ. I have an inheritance from the King of the Universe, which means not only that I get to spend eternity with my Creator but that I am able to walk in the reality that He is mine and I am His.

It means I am able to broker His kingdom here on earth. My life is renewed because I am a son, and I have been set free and have been called according to His purpose.

This reality is available to every lost son and daughter.

When my mom told me she wanted to write this book, I was apprehensive, as it would bring up painful memories of a time that would be easier to forget. Still, I am grateful for her work on this book, and I know that her heart for writing it is that it will encourage families who are walking through really challenging seasons.

It will be a lifeline.

I am convinced that moms and dads who are worn out and waiting on their lost sons and daughters will find hope in these pages. If you are a mother, father, brother, or sister of a prodigal son or daughter, my prayer is that you battle in prayer and have hope in the Lord's goodness and calling on their life. If you are someone who is a prodigal, my prayer is that the depth of His love would so overshadow you that you are rescued by his goodness.

—*Craig Schultz Jr.*

I remember one night when my parents were battling for my brother. He was yelling at my parents and kind of not really making sense, and my dad started to sing "Lord, you are more precious than silver . . ." under his breath; then my mom started to sing it with him. That was by far one of the most memorable moments in my life of my parents. Their son's life was spiraling out of control, and instead of sitting and sulking or being angry, they both chose to declare who God was. That's one of the main things I took away from my brother's journey.

—*Amanda Schultz Lewis*

Introduction

Those who plant in tears
will harvest with shouts of joy.
—PSALM 126:6 (NLT)

This is not the story I wanted to tell. I wanted to be the vibrant voice of Latina moms everywhere, like a Mexican version of Ree Drummond. Instead of chicken pot pie recipes, I would share the secrets of my yummy brisket tacos, or my mama's breakfast burritos or my grandma Rose's Spanish rice.

I would rather encourage young mamas with stories of the joyful grind of motherhood, the hilarious antics of my five beautiful children, and the snaps of my feisty Silky Yorkie, Coco Chanel.

My Yorkie vacillates between acting the part of a good canine citizen one moment to her full-on Robert DeNiro-of-the-doggy-world behavior the next. One moment she is sweetly greeting a young momma with four little ones in tow, and the next moment she is yelling at a fenced dog who dared to look at her sideways. *You talkin' to me? You talkin' to me? Well, who the heck else are you talkin' to? You talkin' to me? Well, I'm the only one here. Oh yeah? Huh? Okay.* I can hear the thick accent of Cesar Milan's judgments echo in my ears as I pull my naughty girl away from the fence in shame.

These are the stories I wanted to tell. Instead, I am sharing a story I never asked for.

I am the mom of a Prodigal Son.

This was not the God-assignment I wanted, and my son's was not just the run-of-the-mill Prodigal journey because his "journey to a far country" happened in our home. His was a furious, filthy trampling of pig slop, touching every area of our lives.

There was no handbook to help me navigate my way through the crazy storm that descended upon our home. No support group or daily e-newsletter existed for suffering parents of spiritual wanderers. In fact, I came to understand that these parents belonged a super-secret-subculture hidden in plain view. They walk among us in places of darkness and doubt, confused and disoriented. Now we join their ranks.

As we were "hiding," the eroded peace in our eyes revealed the truth of our lives. Telling our vulnerable and painful stories was too risky, but our faces betrayed us. Our eyes revealed the truth of our journey. We were in a brutal and holy struggle for our prodigal son's life.

When the raising-of-godly-children's neat and tidy, airtight math equation goes awry, it is quite painful. While raising our little tribe, we held fast to that unspoken, always present *if-then* statement simply stated: if you raise your children in the Lord → they will follow Him. When this equation painfully drifts, the resulting journey produces shame and isolation.

No amount of liquid foundation and powder can hide the tear-stained streaks on the cheeks of a mom waiting for her child to return home. No brand of mascara can revive the three lonely lashes that remain on her lid.

In 2015 I began to feel a stirring to tell my story. An elbow was nudging me deep inside to help lift the suffering of other moms and dads out there. The temptation was to leave the painful situation in the past and remain in hiding. After all, our son is now restored and whole and healed. He is thriving in every way possible. Having successfully completed his education and fully engaged as a business owner, he found and married a Jesus-loving girl. He is faithfully and beautifully serving God and his family. Together he and his wife recently welcomed their beautiful firstborn baby son.

I'm writing to honor the goodness of God by telling of the days and the miles and the moments of our journey. It's a wholehearted fist pump at the end of a finish line, as well as the starting line of our son's beautiful, God-honoring life. I write to bring glory to the God who did it all.

My desire is not to expose every detail of our beloved son's story but rather to paint with broad strokes, from our vantage point, as those details intersected with our lives. The fine details of his journey are not all mine to tell. I've attempted to strike the balance between over-sharing, which would dishonor our son, and giving enough detail to show that Jesus can do above and beyond all we can think or imagine in the most impossible of situations (from our perspective). He can move beyond the reach of our greatest prayers. He can bring beauty for scorched-earth ashes.

It is my hope to share this story with humility, grace, and dignity and from a place of wholeness, healing, and hope.

I want to preserve and honor the journey.

I want to reach out and hug you, the parent who is suffering the blows of wanderings. I want to tell you to never, ever give up on your child, because God never will. For every friend who is at a loss for words, watching their loved one drift in the devastation, I want to remind you of the power of community and the truth of God's promises. My hope is to strengthen and affirm your waiting season.

So many parents of prodigals struggle with unbelief and disillusionment. The struggle drains them of vision and expectation for what is possible. They live in fear and intimidation in the face of out-of-control circumstances. As they live in the space between the now and the not-yet, I pray this book provides a visitation of grace.

I want to comfort you with the comfort of the God of Luke 15. The One who never gives up looking for lost sons and daughters. The One who is willing to climb through muddy landscapes and hoist a filthy lost sheep on His shoulders back to safety. The One who turns a house upside down and cleans every square inch, including all the dusty corners, in pursuit of a single lost coin. The One who keeps his eye steadily on the horizon, undignified running shoes laced, watching for a priceless lost son.

I'm incredibly committed to provide a safe place for prodigal parents. I want to touch your heart by exposing my own, as together we trust in Jesus. More than anything else, I want to be a trustworthy guide. I want to pull in tight with kindness and understanding and grace and point your hearts toward the hope found in Jesus alone. Jesus is the hope of the world, the hope for your heart, and the hope for your child's future.

I want to encourage you to never give up on your child. Ever.

Back in the day, I received countless church casseroles upon the homecoming of each of my newborn babes, and they were deeply appreciated in those early, sleep-deprived days. Unfortunately, there is no Meal Train for parents who spend sleepless, worried nights waiting for their prodigal. This book is my 9x13 covered in foil and prepared for you in the hope of extending warm, compassionate comfort, handed over your threshold to prop you up with support and nourishment.

Someone is crying tonight. Someone is standing at a deli counter, waiting on their order of thin-sliced roast beef, with isolated and fearful tears streaming down their face, as the deli worker gently hands a paper tissue meant for samples over the counter. I have a box of Kleenex in one hand, and I'm extending the other to hold yours.

Let us, parents of prodigals, grab hands and hold on with the most tender of holding.

—*Rhoda Schultz*

SECTION ONE

Our Story

One

THE SALAD DAYS
The Younger Years

Merriam Webster's definition of Salad Days: *a time of youthful in-experience: "my salad days when I was green in judgment" (William Shakespeare); also: an early flourishing period: heyday.*

> *Although that vow was made in my salad days, when I was green in judgment, I do not regret nor retract one word of it. (Queen Elizabeth II during her Silver Jubilee Loyal Address, referring to her vow to God and her people when she made her 21st birthday broadcast)*

We raised our five beautiful children in the foothills of the Mile-High City. Arvada, Colorado, is a yummy little suburb nestled between Denver and Boulder with a distinct small-town feel. It's our home. Growing up, Craig and I attended the local public schools and loved all things Arvada: Pomona High School, Arvada West High School, Ralston Café, Santeramo's Pizza, the Westminster Mall, and Standley Lake, to name a few of our favorite things.

Craig was blonde and handsome and hailed from a strong, faithful German Lutheran family from Wisconsin, until his family moved to Arvada when he was two years old. As the second in a family of seven, he learned to be hardworking, steady, and resilient. He came to faith in Jesus in his first-grade Sunday school class at Peace Lutheran Church. His parents were loving and selfless. His father was an engineer who took him camping and hiking and fishing and could fix any broken thing under the sun. His mother was a faithful and consistent woman of prayer and study. They introduced me to the very non-Mexican food worlds of Bratwurst and German potato salad.

I grew up a Denver native in a beautiful Pentecostal culture, full of energy and emotion, called the First Spanish Assembly of God, where my grandfather served as pastor. I had wonderful, loving parents and embraced the way of Jesus at a young age. Every spiritual deposit I received in the impressionable years of my childhood remains with me. Every impression of God and His work in humanity came to me through the hands of my godly grandparents, who cared for me daily as my mom worked. My identity was formed and shaped by them. They achieved something formative and lasting in me. They confided truth in me, as though imparting valuable insider information. Their unhurried homes were places of hospitality and healing, relentlessly personal, prayerful, and real.

I wanted my life to be shaped by the same things that shaped theirs: God, Scripture, and prayer. My grandparents were peaceful and attentive and were emotionally available and present every single day. They fully leaned in to serve their congregation and their family. When they saw me, their faces lit up, as though there were no one else in the world they would rather see.

Craig and I were fast friends, drawn to one another's faithfulness and ability to make each other laugh. We met at church, when I was sixteen and he was twenty, and were married three years later in all the bubble-gum pink glory the mid-eighties had to offer. Our newlywed years found us enjoying Colorado, water-skiing, snow-skiing, Keith Green, Mexican food, church life, and family.

Before welcoming children, we lived quiet, faithful, middle-child lives. We served in our own varied roles with huge amounts of peace, trust, and assurance. There was a distinct lack of striving in our every day. We owned a lawn service, and we graduated from our church's lay ministry Bible college. We co-led a small group filled with newly-wedded friends on Thursday evenings and gathered with them again in our "Young Marrieds" class on Sundays. We fully trusted the faithfulness of the Father as we served one another and our church.

Our view of God determined how we walked and lived our life. We believed that He was good. We wholeheartedly believed in the uniqueness of the gospel and its transforming power. We believed He was accessible and loved us uniquely.

Year three brought us our first baby, a girl, and in the next eleven years we welcomed four more amazingly delicious babies. Motherhood and fatherhood were the highest callings of our lives, and we wore the mantle like a perfectly fitted pair of pants. Or, in my case, with back-to-back-to-back babies, a perfectly fitted pair of jeans with an elastic hair tie looped between the metal button and the stretched denim hole.

We lived, breathed, and loved our little tribe of German Browns. German Browns are actually a type of trout found in southern Colorado, but the description fit our littles perfectly.

We belonged to a tight-knit church and school community, and our kids grew up in the pews of the same church their entire childhood. Literally. There is a faded, mauve-colored padded pew with a drool stain from the days when we would lay our kids down on the pews and let them sleep when the Sunday evening service went long past their bedtime. I want that pew. If our church ever gets rid of them, I call the drool-stained pew. I'm nostalgic like that.

Over the years, our friendship roots grew deep within a loving, church-centered community: a mixture of conservative home-school and private Christian school families. Our friends, many of whom remain "our people" decades later, were the best humans around. On Sunday mornings I led worship with a beautiful group of singers with floral dresses, matching under-curled bangs, and doily-collars, as Craig taught Sunday school. And on Sunday evenings we would return to lead 100 little singing cherubs in the kids' choir.

There isn't a classic children's musical that I didn't tackle and teach. To this day the only way I remember the Ten Commandments is by recounting the lyrics of "The Perfect Ten" from Angels Aware! And when looking for a minor prophet I still recount the "Books of the Bible Song" from *Wee Sing Praise*. I can't for the life of me remember where I hid Christmas gifts, but I can recall these lyrics with perfect clarity.

Every Easter I would wear my very own biblical costume and sing Sandy Patti's "Via Dolorosa," as "Jesus" carried the cross through the fan-shaped sanctuary while also carrying a ginormous, foam-covered microphone. We Hosanna'd with little babies in little biblical baby costumes perched on our hips, surrounded by sandaled children running around waving palm branches bigger than their bodies. This was our life.

Every Thursday evening we met with our small group, which wasn't very small at all. We lived and breathed and participated in church community in all its beauty. Our friends were deep waters, and we linked arms and surrounded our kiddos with lots of love and a healthy dose of devoted support. Our community represented everything that was good and lovely about church life. We loved each other and we loved Jesus.

We wrapped our kids in all kinds of love: family, church, and community. The beauty of it all makes me smile.

I lived in the kitchen. I made homemade tortillas and home-baked whole wheat bread with a mill that sounded like a massive jet engine had had landed in my kitchen. Eventually, I moved the mill to the garage to preserve the overall hearing health of my little tribe. I realized it was kinda lame to go through the effort of baking bread with fresh-milled wheat while simultaneously ruining their hearing.

When I wasn't cooking a meal, I was cheering my boys at baseball games or sitting next to piano benches, gently whispering "every good boy deserves fudge" as I pointed to the staff when my children lost their musical way, placing their small hands on the all-white keys of C and G. And I never grew weary of delivering the words of the same worn, memorized books with my reading voice (which my kids noticed was strangely similar to my phone voice). We stretched out the VHS tapes of *Psalty the Singing Songbook, Carman Yo Kidz,* and *Adventures in Odyssey* on the daily. Confession: I was *very* heavy handed with the matching denim outfits. No one was safe. Not even my husband. It was the nineties.

We took our kids camping. Five kids. Camping. Coleman stove breakfasts and dinners. Sandwiches and a bag of chips for lunch. My campsite was the gathering place for breakfast burritos because my burritos contained soul-satisfying ingredients like fried potatoes and chorizo. We enjoyed late-night campfires, hiking, and tangled-kid-style "fishing." At night we wiped down the sticky, dirty, bug-sprayed layer off their bodies, bedded them down, and repeated everything again the next day. There is nothing on this green earth as perfect as a family zipped up in sleeping bags in Rocky Mountain crisp night air after a full day of outdoors-y goodness. Nothing.

While I was busy preparing the next meal, or nursing a baby at the campsite, or balancing a not-yet-trained toddler on the porta-potty, my husband, Craig, was busy being all things Superman: chopping firewood, carrying kids on his back, loading fishing lines, and performing all other outdoor superhero duties.

Craig is the greatest man I know. He provided our kids with all the love you could fit inside a five-foot-nine-inch, muscle-bound body. He was all about that family life. He deftly managed family room wrestling matches and dodge ball tournaments and created homemade BB gun shooting ranges, zip lines, and the most ginormous and extreme backyard play set known to humankind.

Our children were recipients of small daily Scripture verses on 3x5 cards faithfully written out in Craig's distinct all-caps handwriting. He spoke genuine blessings over our children daily and stepped up and leveraged his head-of-the-household authority in the most natural way. Jesus was his joy and his family a close second. He pointed our children toward a good and gracious Father by being one himself. I've had a front row view of this quiet giant of a man for thirty-one years.

He secretly buys jars of liquid cheese and sneaks spoonfuls, incredulously defiling my spreads of homemade Mexican food. Jars of liquid cheese. After all these years, he recently confessed to me that white people like chorizo but aren't as crazy about corn tortillas as I think they should be. This from someone who likes liquid cheese. It's iron sharpening iron. Every single day.

Our world felt entirely safe and secure.

Craig Jr. was the second born of our tribe of five. Like his older sister, he decided to gestate beyond the reasonable forty-week mark and kept me comfy and cozy with my swollen feet barely fitting into winter socks and boots while his remained firmly lodged in my rib cage.

Overall, my pregnancies were ridiculously easy, and I was struck with baby fever something awful. I'm not saying I had easy deliveries. They were more of a long, drawn-out showdown between my contraction-print-out-receipt-looking thingy that measured their duration and frequency and the actual, snail-paced dilation. Slow and steady always won the showdown, no matter what story the labor monitor printout was telling.

It didn't matter, because I always fell ridiculous, head over heels in love with the impending little person, not to mention that I rather enjoyed the baby years because: stretchy pants. I truly believe that stretchy pants are the single greatest mom invention of the twentieth century. I never gave in to the pressure of losing the "baby weight" between my babies, thanks to the unspoken lack of honesty between moms and stretchy pants. Life is hard: wear stretchy pants.

Craig Jr. entered the world, thanks to the grace of God and the miracle-working powers of Pitocin, at eight pounds of unreasonable amounts of beauty. Truly. All newborns are a miraculous sight to behold, but this one was actually beautiful from day one.

He was easy to love and rambunctious from the start. I was going through some old boxes recently and came across a handwritten note from him when he was small: "I love you mom. You make me fall in love. You cook good food."

It was such joy to watch him grow. To wonder what kind of man he would be. If something could be climbed, he would climb it. If a rock could be thrown, he would throw it. He scaled door jambs like a spider monkey and perched himself high above my reach inside the frame with his front leg forward as he leveraged his weight on his back leg.

I remember holding him in my arms, his perfect white skin against my brown, looking at his beautiful eyes and kissing his delicious, chubby hands. The smell of smashed banana in his grip and the memory of counting his fingers and toes will never fade. The amount of love I had for him couldn't be contained, and I squeezed every drop out of every single day.

I love little boy pictures of him so much I think my face might explode.

We welcomed three more children after him: two hysterically funny and sweet brothers and a spicy baby sister for the finale. I delighted in watching people's expressions fade to borderline panic at the grocery store when they saw my pregnant situation waddle down the cereal aisle with all my little ducklings in a not-so-tidy row. Two were "mostly" staying beside me, one safely contained in the baby seat, one in my arms, and one in my belly. As I approached, I could literally see their faces shift from curious amusement to an uncomfortable inner struggle as they wondered if they should offer "help."

Craig Jr. took us on a wild ride of action-packed adventure. He was in a terrible rush to go just about everywhere. I watched in horror after my husband removed the training wheels on his toddler-sized bicycle, as three-year-old Craig Jr. gleefully exploded up the street with his miniature muscle-bound legs, powering the smallest bike you've ever seen up our hill. He was a quick learner and excelled in every sport we dared to sign him up for. He was full of all possibility and potential. He was outstanding and smart and creative.

If I could save time in a bottle, I would slow it down and relive every single one of his baseball/gymnastics/basketball/football moments. By the time he was in high school, he was an All-Conference, All-State, All-Everything football champion. During his senior year alone he rushed for 35 touchdowns and over 1,200 yards.

He was gifted in every way.

Together with his siblings, we were his number one fans. My husband and I would speak only to each other during his games, leaving no margin for chit-chat with our fellow fans. I couldn't even handle sitting in the bleachers with the crowd. We started the games in the stadium seats, pretending to be normal citizens, but were quickly pulled by a magnetic force to pacing up and down the sidelines lest we hurt ourselves.

To put it mildly, I lost my ever-loving mind at every single one of his football games. I actually felt morning-after soreness on Saturday mornings from my Friday night pacing with every single muscle of my body and teeth in a knotted mess of euphoric worry and joy. The struggle was real. Real good, that is.

We knew our children would approach faith in Jesus differently, just as some of them preferred scrambled eggs and others over-medium, and we recognized their differences along the way. We listened and took note of the nuance and uniqueness of each child's life. We understood that the stakes were high, and we embraced the calling with all our hearts.

Our kids were fun and our kids were funny.
Ours was not a serious and sober household of faith,
but one filled with fall-down-funny moments.

Three-year-old at the dinner table, with a voice distinct and scratchy like Vito Corleone: "What is the date?"

Me: "April 24th."

Three-year-old: "Oh, this is the day Cain killed Abel."

Me: (gobsmacked) "Um. I don't think we actually know the date when Cain killed Abel."

Three-year-old: "Yep, it was April 24th."

I cannot wait to get to heaven and ask Jesus the exact date when Cain killed Abel. Can. Not. Wait.

I drove a white conversion van with matted-down carpet and faux wood-paneled interior. There's no shame in this. The van represented what a glorious, sticky, full-throttle life we were living. At the end of each week I drove that bad boy to the car wash and vacuumed the tacky evidence of the weekly meals and snacks that had taken place in the van while driving to piano lessons, baseball practice, Awana, soccer games, and a host of church activities. The corners of the van held all manner of crumbs and empty tubes of Girl Scout cookie sleeves, hardened sandwich crusts, half-full sippy cups, wrappers, flyers, and every manner of book and bag imaginable.

Never once did we fear one of our children would stray from their faith. Having both survived our teenage years as godly kids, preserving our parents from pain, we honestly assumed our kids would do the same. We were wise enough to know that we weren't parenting experts, but we simply loved Jesus, loved each other, and loved our kids.

We lived in willing submission to Jesus and believed our children would learn to submit to His authority by observing our lives. We were filled with faith, and we recognized that spiritual groundwork is laid early in life and doesn't always look very spiritual. It takes place at breakfast. At lunch. At dinner. During backyard play. On the baseball fields.

We were always teaching, and they were always watching and learning.

Our daily attempts to identify and correct sinful behavior were laced with the good news of Jesus, guiding our children toward reconciliation and supporting their child-sized faith. Our attempts at warnings and corrections were always framed as an invitation into something better.

We invited our children into something beautiful, beyond duty-laden rule following. As something we were genuinely experiencing ourselves, we were merely tearing pieces off our own daily bread and passing them around the table.

We fully trusted the faithfulness of the Father as we served our family, our church, and our community. Our family culture was shaped by gracious love. Connected to Jesus not just for salvation but for an ongoing love relationship.

We felt called in our parenting journey.

We put our trust in the God who called us to lead our little tribe. Ultimately, we trusted He would accomplish what He called us to do. We were steadfast.

Faithful is He who calls you, and He also will bring it to pass.
—1 THESSALONIANS 5:24 (NASB)

We lived a life anchored to this great promise. Our trust was rooted in Him, not merely in ourselves. We understood that we couldn't give what we didn't have, so we just kept pressing forward into Jesus.

We believed the Bible was given to us to reveal God's character and purposes for humanity and to show us how to live. We still do. We depended on it as we shepherded the hearts of our children.

We had our fair share of tyrannical toddler moments, for sure, and we understood the need to win in the little moments before they became big ones. We didn't really know what a "big moment" would look like, but we understood the concept. During the young years, we recognized that all children have some level of appetite to self-rule. Some more mild and some stronger-willed. We were blessed with a healthy mix of both.

Our church community effortlessly provided help, authority, and advice. We all wanted to grow God-loving kids, and our life-on-life relationships created a natural flow in which help and advice came in the form of story and experience with other godly parents. Community allowed us to leverage other trusted voices and accomplish more than we could have alone.

Community is good and messy.
Community is good and pleasant.

Each family had its distinct flavor: some families were more conservative and anti-TV than others. Some more sporty and less book-ish. Some were secret Disney watchers, and some were secret Barbie doll owners. Some were dress-wearing Gothard-ites, and others were "put-your-kids-in-a-classroom and sip a cup of coffee in your stretchy pants while they are gone for a few hours, for goodness sake." It was all good.

God gave us the beautiful opportunity of parenting in the context of community. We were not parenting alone. Our challenges and difficulties were beautifully shared.

It goes without saying that the early, sweet years built a solid foundation for all of our children to firmly stand. There was no small amount of honest-to-goodness pride attached to being a "good family." The whole lot of us worked diligently toward the mission God had called us into, which was raising good, solid kids.

Before the world of parenting blogs and pins, we lived uncomplicated lives, with a distinct lack of comparison. We absorbed and savored each day with a deep understanding (beyond our years) that we were living the sweet years—or "salad days," as my husband now refers to them.

Two

"I HAVE A BAD FEELING ABOUT THIS"
The High School Years

I don't like scary movies one bit. I cover my eyes and ears and cower when horror movie previews and commercials sneak their way into my space. The sensation of something bad, very bad, lurking around every corner is dreadful to me rather than thrilling.

There is a sense of foreboding in the early stages of your prodigal child's journey that is the most unsettling feeling of all.

Beyond a mere loss of control, with every small rumbling you get this strange feeling in the pit of your stomach that says, "I have a bad feeling about this."

Something is "off" in the formerly green and simple landscape of your comfortable world, leaving you with an ever-so-subtle hint of unrest, fear, anxiety, and instability. The reassuring and familiar paths are strangely hidden. The resulting suspense and uncertainty leave you with the worst kind of spiritual motion sickness.

By the time our son was in middle school, he was a confident leader: he served as a student leader at his Christian school's weekly chapel gatherings and on several of our church's middle school missions trips to Mexico and Scotland. Without fear, he boldly preached the gospel message on the streets of Ireland at the age of fourteen. He was brave and open hearted, soft toward the Lord and toward his family.

He led worship at the middle school's chapel services with a black oversized acoustic guitar. Like Johnny Cash. I love that guitar. We still have it, and I dream of the day my grandchildren pick it up and strum a worship song.

He went through a phase when he wore a puka-shell necklace with a single guitar pick woven into it, and we "frosted the tips" of his brown hair. Raise your hand and say "amen" if you remember those days.

His teachers marveled at his academic excellence, leadership qualities, and overall chutzpah. He never met a challenge he wasn't willing to conquer with absolute confidence. His inexperience with football in the eighth grade did not deter him from attacking the sport and succeeding in every way.

**He was extraordinary and remarkable beyond his years.
Marked for greatness.**

He had a huge heart, on and off the field, and was the center of a veritable social swarm of butterflies. I once heard a swarm of butterflies described as a kaleidoscope, which described our middle-school-aged kaleidoscope of a people-person son most perfectly. He. Loved. People.

He also loved his brothers and sisters with the white-hot fires of a thousand suns. Many epic moments in our family lore include campfires. A family favorite is the time Craig Jr. dove across the fire to scoop little toddler brother out of the coals, saving him from a fiery demise. It was truly a superhero Dash (Disney's *Incredibles*) moment. Before we could even see the toddler falling, Craig Jr. had snatched his tiny body.

Not only was he brave, but he was tender with his brothers and sisters and was never, ever, harsh with them. He led with a huge, compassionate heart, and he wisely saved his toughness and strength for sports, never once rough with his siblings.

It was obvious he was going to be a strong, bold, courageous, compassionate, and determined leader who would extend the kingdom of God on this earth. God was moving in his life. Big. His fingerprints of faithfulness were all over our son, and he was experiencing God's grace and power in deeply personal ways.

As we entered his high school years, the horizon looked promising in every way. He began his tenth-grade year on top of the world. He truly loved his teachers and friends, and his grades remained strong as he threw himself into all things football, because football was life. He was steady as they come and was always showing up. By the end of his tenth-grade football season, he was named "spiritual leader" of his team.

**Around the same time, the first tiny
rumblings began to be felt.**

He was a true and good friend. The kind of friend that most teenagers don't even know how to be. He was all about celebrating others and was uniquely thoughtful and generous. But his social popularity, excellence on the field, and favor with older teammates came with a high price.

He found himself in a precarious social world with older teammates whose life choices more than edged toward the dark side of healthy Christian student life. His teammates were drawn to him and became somewhat of an "extended family" in his heart. The attention and acceptance from these older boys was a heady experience for Craig Jr., and (we now know) he was exposed to not-so-innocent amounts of alcohol and drug abuse at off-the-grid teammate gatherings.

Here's where our naiveté played an early guilty role in the unseen mudslide around the bend. Our inexperience with a student athlete in a Christian school led us to view the company he kept with rose-colored glasses. We assumed things we should have never assumed. We failed to gut-check things we should have gut-checked. We assumed the best, and we failed.

Combine our all-around successful teenage boy inexperience

with his *amazing* track record leading up to this point, and you have the ingredients for potential slippage.

It was not his intention to slide sideways down a mudslide of sin; it was more like an imperceptibly slow mud leak. All the while he continued to thrive as a successful high school student and athlete with strong conviction and character. It was sneaky. I dare say it was an adventure.

It wasn't some huge decision to slip into a world of bad company. It was subtle. It was one friendship at a time. One weekend at a time.

Catch the foxes for us,
the little foxes
that spoil the vineyards,
for our vineyards are in blossom.
—SONG OF SOLOMON 2:15 (ESV)

The rumblings presented themselves in an ever so slight pulling away from us. At times our eye contact was slightly diminished. Closeness and genuine laughter became more rare than normal. The funny remembering and telling of epic family connection stories at the dinner table faded. He seemed distracted. At times he was slightly moody, withdrawn, and disconnected.

A quiet teenager can be the loudest sound on earth.

Over the next two years of high school, these small cues rose and fell, like the currents of the sea. At times we felt a hopeful surge of reconnection and spiritual spark. At other times we were filled with an unsettling dread. There were stretches of genuine respectful connection, and at other times an unusual pulling back from us. He maintained a high GPA and continued to thrive in his activities, but something was off.

He remained connected with his siblings, but the continental drift of their innocent world pushed it further and further from his new frontier. It was as though he was standing on an ice shelf that had recently broken away from the shore, slowly drifting, and his siblings were standing on the edge of the shore. Close enough to play, but with greater and greater effort.

The slipping away was also magnified by curious doubts on his side: he began to express doubts like "Did God really say that?" and challenge us with statements like "My so-and-so teacher or youth leader says there's nothing wrong with this or that." Our family convictions were a bit more conservative than our son's youth leaders and teachers.

The liberty and exposure he found in his last two years of high school undermined his upward trajectory of "doing what is right" out of a love relationship with Jesus by the seemingly harmless downward pull of "doing what he pleased." He was exploring a new world of adventure that appeared to have more satisfying, wider boundaries of freedom but was actually leading him toward smallness.

Perhaps he, like Adam and Eve, began to believe the lies of the enemy, suspecting that God had been "keeping something from him."

It was a confusing season. For all of us.

Our landscape was shifting, and we were bewildered and out of sorts. I was pushing hard against the sensation of something sinister lurking around the corner. Our attempts at discipline and connection and reconnection were strangely missing the mark, and although I was more than a little unsettled I absolutely 100% believed this was a "phase" that would soon pass.

Three

DENIAL

"This Is Absolutely Not Happening"

"**B**ack in the day"—one of my favorite terms, by the way—young mamas used to cook with recipes from cookbooks featuring *no* pictures. I know. Crazy.

Picture-free cookbooks take me back to the days of handwritten mail and postcards from unseen loved ones. Days of returning from vacation and taking your film to the film counter and the anticipation of enjoying the images. Of sitting down to a delicious meal and fully savoring the engaged faces and conversation. Spiral notebooks. Mix tapes and LPs. *Don't even get me started on my album collection, because Carole King's* Tapestry *was my life.* Sitting down in a hallway tethered to the twisted and stretched phone cord around the corner from the kitchen as you talked with your friends. Days of not seeing someone's face for ages and ages and then reuniting with them.

Back to cookbooks.

My favorite, well-worn go-tos are my vintage cookbooks from the sixties and seventies. I've read these old girls cover-to cover many times and have left my messy, splattered mark on their well-worn pages.

Sometimes I would *(gasp)* check them out from the library and *(gasp)* handwrite the recipes on cards to save for later. This was our crazy pre-internet world. As my littles were in the kids' section, selecting their weekly bundles, I would hide myself in the DDC 640: Home & Family Management section. DDC is short for Dewey Decimal Classification System. *Does this still even exist?*

I would lose myself in worlds of dishes never prepared by my mother, aunties, and grandmothers. Exotic meals like "Chicken a la King" and "California Ham Supreme." One of my favorite discoveries was "Swedish Meat Balls." I adore a recipe that ends with "Into fat left in skillet, stir flour, 1 teaspoon sugar, 1 ¼ teaspoon salt, pepper; slowly add water, cream; and stir until thickened." Any day you finish a meal by adding to the "fat left in skillet" is a good day. After my family cleaned up every last morsel, I would wipe up the caramelized gravy from the skillet with a warm tortilla before washing it, because Swedish Meat Balls are better with tortillas, right?

After a few seasoned years, I could simply "look" at a recipe and visualize its final product. I could tell by the ingredients how well its taste and texture would appeal to my family. I could determine the cost per serving at a glance. I had a running mental list of my pantry goods and could easily take inventory of my shopping list needs to complete just about any recipe I considered. I was like a human Buzzfeed sifting through my own fast-forward clip of every step until I reached the end product.

By the time my oldest son became a teenager, I expected the same Buzzfeed superpowers in parenting. I just *knew* my kids would be fine. I *fully* expected them to be healthy and whole. I was present for each and every ingredient that we added to the bowl and was taste testing along the way.

I was certain that the last two years of Craig's up-and-down high school experimenting would right themselves with the fresh start of college. A change of landscape would reset his trajectory. I just *knew* it.

Fresh starts were the answer to all things gone awry. Loss of interest in your Bible reading plan? Start a new one. Loss of order in your kitchen junk drawer? Toss the contents overboard and start afresh. Better yet, buy a few drawer organization trays from Target, and the fresh start will actually work. Fresh starts are always the answer.

I was wrong.

The eighteen months following Craig's high school graduation were an epic free fall. His first three semesters of college were filled with failing grades, dropped classes, and a change of school every semester in an attempt to start over. Uncharacteristic episodes and interactions left us with the most unsettling dread.

**We couldn't see through the sea of red flags
that were popping up left and right.**

His first semester of college felt as though we were off on the wrong foot from the very first step. The subfloor of each semester continued to slip and slip until there was nothing left underfoot. At the end of the first semester, we transferred his (few transferrable) credits and began his winter semester at a different campus. Again, he quickly lost his footing, and we were back where we had started.

After his second failed semester, he desperately threw away his phone in the hope of losing contact with all unsavory connections. He sat in our front room, reading his Bible, pressing into the Lord, making a huge attempt on his own to regain his footing. But the undertow was strong, and he slowly slipped back under its current.

For his third semester we attempted a community college. Same lost footing. With every failed semester we continued to believe the change of location and fresh start would be the answer.

During this free-fall season, Craig Jr. confessed to his dad that he was addicted to marijuana.

He couldn't concentrate in college and desperately wanted to stop the habit. He really needed our help, so we ran to a Christian counselor like thirsty beggars with cups in our hands. These counseling sessions led to prescription antidepressants, which in turn caused unbalanced emotions.

It was the worst cycle imaginable.

It was the beginning of something I didn't fully understand or anticipate. I watched a few tiny ripples grow into a dangerous storm of destruction, and we were left holding a small, torn plastic bag over our heads for shelter. I felt a sickness I had never felt before, like the worst flu ever.

I have *no* expertise in these matters, but our doctor informed us that the impact of marijuana on a teenage brain can be vastly different from that on a fully grown adult. No two bodies are exactly the same, and therefore the effects of substances are unique to the individual. For us the effect was life altering.

Depression, insomnia, and anxiety took seats at our table. Stronger drugs and alcohol pulled up two extra chairs. Unwanted, rude guests with no regard for our family and for the son we were so desperately fighting for.

I now felt as though a 400-pound man were sitting on my chest. An ugly, strange compression pressed against my worried, weary heart, cracking it open. Everything inside my chest was splitting apart and turning upside down, like a toy my children used to play with.

Remember the plastic, blue and red Tupperware ball with yellow shapes inside? The one where you pulled the yellow side handles and yellow plastic circles and stars and squares and ovals would spill out everywhere as you gently guided small hands in putting it back together?

That was me. Completely spilled out.

When our son was clear-headed and sober, he was respectful and connected to us, but when he was under the influence of a substance, or suffering the negative effects of the antidepressant, he was a tangled mess of hostility and confusion.

It was as though our strong, beloved, remarkable son were being held hostage, and we continued to attempt to meet the demands for ransom, only to have him moved to another location and held again. The spiritual sickness of drug and alcohol abuse was met with the physical sickness of anxiety and depression. Over and over this cycle continued.

This is not happening.

In addition to wreaking havoc on his education, the abuse and anxiety swung around like a wrecking ball unleashed against the peace of our home, with no regard for victims. Since Craig Jr. was living at home during this season, his siblings witnessed angry, confused outbursts followed by sullen periods of depression, followed by respectful behavior. This cycle repeated itself over and over. We were all held hostage to this strange invader.

Our wide-eyed children sometimes witnessed dramatic scenes as we pleaded with their brother, and fought with him, and fought *for* him. We loved him so much that we became desperate, and our desperation took front and center stage to our accustomed family dynamic. We were trying so hard to pull him back, and there were many moments when he grabbed the rope and tried to make his way back to us.

We pulled our children tight and instinctively clasped our arms around them, as you would in a storm-tossed boat. We constantly confirmed our love for their older brother and for them. We assured them he would be fine, and they believed us.

**I was still not prepared to settle
for this trajectory and say, "Well, that's just
the way it is. Lots of teenagers stray."**

The raising of our children was my life's work. We were really good parents and had a really good life. He was going to turn out fine. More than fine. I was confident he was still going to be a strong and courageous man of God.

At the same time that my heart refused to give up, I felt as though I were having a nervous breakdown.

Sometimes there was pain, and other times there was frustration. Sometimes it was just a tasteless, dull melancholy that settled over me like a thick cloud. I was sad for my son, for my husband, our other children, and myself.

Our desperate failed attempts with Christian counselors and

new schools left me in my own funk of denial. Peeling back the layers of denial can reveal a nasty root called pride.

Our family life had been sweetly satisfying before this storm. We were truly a sweet and happy family, and we enjoyed a good life. A good family is a good thing, but it's not the ultimate thing. I was grieving the loss of the goodness we had once experienced. In addition to my brokenhearted state on behalf of my son, I felt sorry for myself, and my self-sadness was a direct result of pride.

Prodigal journeys are seasons of revealing.

At this point in the journey, my pride created a conflict of interest for my prodigal child. It kept me stuck in denial and distracted from reclaiming the life and future of our son. It denied me the grace I was praying for every day.

> *But he gives us more grace. That is why Scripture says: 'God opposes the proud, but shows favor to the humble.'*—JAMES 4:6 (NIV)

I was attempting to stand whole and rally around my family by faith while simultaneously pacing the floor, wringing my hands, repeating, "This is absolutely not happening."

Pride clouded my thinking and blocked my view from seeing His fingerprints of faithfulness all over my son, because I was wasting time shaking my fists in the air at the injustice of the whole situation. I missed the invitation to make a list of all the amazing things God had done as I busied myself filling pages with lists of all the reasons this should not be happening.

While you are painting protest signs to wave in front of the Lord, precious time is wasted.

If you spend all your days bemoaning the lost ground, you will miss the valuable opportunities each day to gain ground with your prodigal child.

This prodigal season is about *your* heart as much as it is about your child's heart. Craig Jr. needed to see me living a gospel-humble life every single day, pointing him to the nearness of the Father's love, but instead he saw me conflicted with self-pity and pride.

Your faith will get stuck in the muddy waters of self-pity if you remain in denial.

Here's another fun byproduct of pride: isolation. Remember that vibrant community I described in the Salad Days? Well, I pulled back in the biggest way ever. I gave in to the temptation to withdraw and drift into isolation and slowly cut myself off from vibrant social interaction and engagement. I went into hiding. I held my lifelong friends at a distance. I stiff-armed my opposition before any support could be extended.

Our small-group community was good and authentic and healthy. However, I sensed a hint of danger in exposing our reality. My own flaws and failures and pride led me to distrust the possibility of exposure. In isolation, I spared myself from even a hint of rejection, disapproving glances, or condemning whispers.

Isolation was a way of self-preservation, and it was a way of exerting a small amount of control in the midst of an out-of-control situation.

I became a professional stealthy, slippery latecomer and early departer at any and all church services. I stopped asking friends to come over for dinners and game nights and declined any invitations to the same. While I continued engagement in immediate family gatherings, I stopped short of meaningful connection with non-family members.

Isolation is never the solution to deep pain and adversity, but here I was, frantically trying to bind my wounds in any way I could think of, and one of the fixes seemed to apply the seemingly safe bandage of isolation.

This was my first immersion in silence and solitude. Not the good kind of silence and solitude that provide a backdrop to devotion, but the kind that made me feel more alone than I'd ever felt. Isolation will leave you with a devastating loneliness and only serves to make you more anxious about your situation.

Like my son, I have always been a people person. I love good friends, good food, and good conversation, where the walls drip with loyalty and safety and laughter and shared memories. I love, love, LOVE lifting my voice in worship in close proximity with others. I could do it for days on end without tiring. Big Group Living was one of my most favorite things.

But our close friends were in the same stage of life, and no one seemed to be struggling with their teens. I was shamefully alone— and alone with my shame.

There is a huge benefit to being in relationship with people who find themselves a little further down the parenting road than yourself. However, since parents of prodigals tend to move through seasons under a super-secret cloaking device, these fellow parents were hidden from us, which only served to reinforce my isolation.

Cloaking devices are a technology utilized by certain species to render starships, stations, equipment, personnel and even planets invisible to the naked eye and/or sensors.—STAR TREK WIKI FANSITE

Did I mention I am both a Trekkie *and* a Star Wars fan? We can talk about the difference in fan bases later.

Here's what I've learned: once said family is safely out of danger, they release the cloaking device, give thanks for the season's end, and move ahead with a big sigh.

Nobody knows it even happened.

Cloaked and alone, I had silently slipped from the phase of "pretending everything is okay" to the darkness of realizing it absolutely was not. I can now see that my pride and denial were ways of digging in my heels in an attempt to keep this situation from moving forward.

I once had a child dig in his heels and refuse to go to the fourth grade. He made himself freakishly heavy when we tried to pick him up and load him into the van. He clung to the edges of the doors with sticky Spiderman strength, and he even bolted out the back door during breakfast as I was giving him a "pep talk" before loading time. All of his heel digging couldn't stop the inevitable from happening: the child eventually faced the fourth grade.

During my painful denial/pride/isolation cycle I realized the most profound truth: our children are not made to meet all of our emotional needs. I "knew" this to be true, but now I was experiencing that truth in the worst way.

Your child's wanderings have no regard for your reputation.

The one who will suffer the most if you stay in this denial/pride/ isolation phase too long is your prodigal child. The enemy uses these tactics to keep you from fully paying attention and fully leaning into the God who can heal and change the course of your child's heart.

I wish I could paint a more flattering portrait of myself during this season. I wish I could say that I was in step with the Spirit from the beginning. For each parent of a prodigal, this early season of peeling back the layers of denial and revealing the ugly roots of pride is where relationships break down. Oftentimes, parents resent this hard cultivation process and, feeling as though they've already sacrificed and sown into their children enough to last a lifetime, disengage from this brutal work.

Many families withdraw from their wandering child and enter a season of estrangement that can last for years.

We were all in.

Three failed semesters of college. Confessions of drug and alcohol addiction. Prescription antidepressants. Massive confusion, anxiety, and disorder.

An entire painful season peeling back the layers of denial, revealing the roots of pride and slipping further into isolation.

Four

THE "F" WORD
Failure

We moms and dads have a very real aversion to the "F" word. We don't like the slippery slope of "freaking" or "flipping," either, because they're too darn close to the real deal, and you never know what might spill out.

Even worse, the harshest "F" word of all: "failure."

Like all other parents, prodigal parents take on the failure or success of their children as their identity. With every day it became clearer that we were failing. Badly. As time passed our joyful dinner table dynamic was reduced to worried, funky meals, with our son's strained relationship sitting front and center.

We spent an entire sad Thanksgiving wondering where he was, making excuses to the extended family for his absence. Worried and sad.

To say you "lose sight of the shore" while your prodigal child is wandering is a massive understatement. I couldn't even remember what the shore looked like, but I had a distant recollection that it included laughter and sunlight.

Why are you cast down O my soul,
and why are you in turmoil within me?
Hope in God; for I shall again praise him,
my salvation and my God.—PSALM 42:5–6 (ESV)

During this dark, fearful season of uncertainty, our precious oldest daughter became engaged to a wonderful young man. Laughter and sunlight pierced through the clouds.

Two months after the worried and sad Thanksgiving it was President's Day, and our daughter's boyfriend invited my husband for a Starbucks. We suspected the motive for the coffee invitation had something to do with his newfound worship pastor position, combined with our daughter's impending college graduation in May.

Craig set aside his troubled, overwhelming worry over our son and gave his full attention to our daughter's boyfriend. He had a feeling this coffee invitation was going to be significant.

Life continues to happen during your prodigal child's wandering season. Life in all its beautiful, simple, extraordinary unfolding. Holidays continue. Baseball season comes and goes. Young love blooms. It doesn't all come to a grinding halt.

What transpired at the small, round Starbucks table became a hallowed meeting between two men. Two men who loved the same girl. One father and one future husband. A sacred impartation of blessing. A confirmation of acceptance and a profound exchange of wisdom and love. The beginnings of release.

He asked for her hand in marriage. My husband loosened his grip and placed her sweet hand firmly in his. Our oldest, precious firstborn child was getting married.

Later that evening, after the Starbucks meeting, we waited in the car for our youngest, our little ten-year old daughter, who at any moment would come skipping out of her evening dance class, knowing that she would be wearing the cutest little dance tights, carrying her small pencil bag, and loving that the content of her pencil bag was none other than a single tube of lip gloss. We sat in measured calm and reflected on the beauty of our oldest daughter's life and her hopeful future. More laughter. More sunlight.

Two stories were unfolding at the same time. A daughter beginning her own family journey. A son on a confusing and treacherous journey. Our love for both of them beautifully and painfully deep.

I broke the calm with some fairly large gulps of tears and finally sank my face in my hands and said, "I'm going to miss her so much."

From the moment I'd first held my firstborn daughter, I'd felt some kind of ancient shift inside, locking me into what I was made to be. Calling me to my own self. I was meant to be a mom, and the journey of motherhood that began with the simple compass of those gorgeous brown eyes continues to this very moment.

I knew I would miss her so much. Although it was a completely selfish thought, I must admit to feeling it. As she spread her wings and flew from my nest to prepare her own, mine would be missing such a profound piece. This selfish thought was balanced with hopeful, honest joy for her new marriage and family journey. In the midst of a storm, sunlight.

These feelings of daring to relax in the sun's warm rays would quickly be interrupted by the most jarring news of all.

The evening after their engagement, our son was arrested.

A confused, tangled roadside fight turned upside down, and as a result several counts were leveled against our son.

While basking in the sweet afterglow of the engagement festivities, Craig and I were sharing a smothered burrito at our favorite North Denver Mexican food dive. We were discussing wedding details when we received a call from our son, who was in the Arvada jail, informing us of the incident and that he would be transferred to the county jail later that evening.

Let that sink in for a minute.

I sat with my hands over my mouth, burrito untouched, as my husband ran out the door and left me to pay the bill.

As Craig drove away, he called the county jail and was crushed to learn that we couldn't see our son that evening and that he would be spending the night in jail. He was informed of the bail amount, which we could deliver the next morning.

Bail amount. These two words were now in our lives. Our son was spending the night in jail, and we were gathering bail funds. Wedding plans and bail amounts.

Our whole world tilted, and we were walking on uneven ground. It was like an amusement park ride, where we had forgotten to take our motion-sickness medication, and for extra effect pillowcases were pulled over our faces, obstructing our view. Sounds were muffled. Our sense of direction was fuzzy. We fumbled to steady ourselves on handrails that didn't exist.

We couldn't even sleep, knowing our son was spending a traumatic night in jail. Instead, we tossed and turned and waited for morning. I considered parking outside the jail to wait until the doors opened in the morning, but my husband took charge and held back the crazy.

"Holding Back the Crazy," by the way, is a muscle my husband often flexed during this season. He deserves a medal for this activity alone. The man is a saint.

When Craig Jr. was released the following morning, we were certain this would all be quickly behind us, that the charges would have been some sort of terrible mistake. We were *certain* his lack of any kind of "record" would work in our favor. We would all move forward, and our son would have learned a hard lesson.

We were certain.

When we received the police report of the incident, an ugly hysteria made its way to the surface, and I couldn't actually read it. I made it through a paragraph and handed it back to my husband. My reaction was both too big and too small, a simultaneous overreacting and underreacting. To this day I've never read the entire account.

After the arrest, our son was determined to wean himself off the antidepressants, certain they contributed to the situation. We were all concerned about even worse side effects from the weaning. It felt like a lose/lose scenario.

The day after his release we began our daily calls to a court-ordered drug testing line and enrolled him in a county-ordered extensive substance abuse evaluation. Drug testing lines. Substance abuse evaluations.

**Further study of the court documents indicated that
if he missed a drug test or committed a small misdemeanor
he would automatically face two years of jail time.**

Certainly, he would *not* miss a drug test. We were calling every morning to make sure that base was covered. Certainly, he would *not* commit a small misdemeanor. The warning and consequences were loud and clear.

Long, ugly story short, he continued to walk down a reckless path. We were warning him hard. The court system warned him hard. But his cycle of behavior remained unchanged. Same crowd. Same behavior. Grief upon grief. Loss upon loss.

Then one fateful night, as though our broken hearts could handle one more thing, we received a call from the local police.

The most gracious local policeman you can imagine was on the other end of the line, telling us that our son had received a DUI. The officer assured us that he was very cooperative and polite, and we could come to the Arvada jail and pick him up.

Just like that.

In total silence I pulled on my jeans and gathered what remained of my thinning hair in a ponytail. I watched my weary husband quietly put his wallet in his jeans pocket, and we drove to the Arvada jail without saying a word.

As we drove, I rolled down the window for some too-cold fresh air. The streets were dark and empty. Red blinking stoplights and dark, empty parking lots.

Just like that. Small misdemeanor. Check. Automatic two years of jail time. Check.

I felt dull and heavy and thick. My brain couldn't comprehend where this was going. My courage had reached its limit. I could have easily gone my whole life without knowing the limit, but now I knew exactly where the boundary lay, and I desperately wanted to crawl back over the chalk line to the world I had known before this moment.

So now, in addition to the court appearances for the charges related to the roadside fight there were separate and additional court appearances relating to the DUI. Instead of cheering for my strong and brave son on the sidelines of a high school field, I was now sitting in courtrooms and drug-testing centers witnessing his future unfold in surreal measures of time.

Failure.

The bottom ground to this failure seemed to know no end. When would this descending elevator come to a grinding halt? When would there be no more available levels? Surely this battle-worn building of failure had a basement.

For the next few months our summer days were spent driving our son to the county courthouse for various hearings. Meeting our daughter to visit venues for her wedding. Making dinner for our three younger children. Checking on drug tests for our son. Visiting florists with our daughter. Spraying sunscreen on our young children at the pool. On and on the cycle continued. The extremes of these situations were not lost upon us.

Gathering yellow shapes and stuffing them
back into the blue and red every evening.
Cracking it open every single morning. Spilling out.

During visits to the courthouse and court-ordered drug checks, I came face-to-face with more ugly heart issues I'd never suspected I had. This season seemed to be a clean sweep of unseen and unidentified heart issues. I felt disdain. Disdain for the "reckless men and women" sitting in the chairs at the drug-testing centers, waiting for their numbers to be called. Disdain instead of compassion. Disdain for broken users and abusers. Disdain for those who pulled their exhausted families through muddy landscapes to sit, worried, in plastic chairs.

I saw weary, elderly moms sitting next to grown adult sons. Both broken. Both weary.

I knew they needed rest for their souls. So did we. My son was tired and weary—I could see it. He was worn out and hurting. I was worn out and hurting.

"Come to me, all who labor and are heavy laden, and I will give you rest. Take my yoke upon you, and learn from me, for I am gentle and lowly in heart, and you will find rest for your souls. For my yoke is easy, and my burden is light."—MATTHEW 11:28–30 (ESV)

I was sitting in chairs with weary, hurting people whose faces showed deep lines of story. Stories of loss and hopelessness. But, instead of opening wide my arms with compassion and tenderness, I folded my arms and held them in superior contempt. I was filled with self-righteous entitlement. I didn't deserve to be here.

What kind of a person was I? What kind of a Christ-follower would feel such things?

Me.

Slowly, I peeled off the judgments and superiorities like a heavy winter jacket in the middle of summer, relieving myself of the weight. *Lord, put to death the sinful judgments of my heart. I confess the filth of discrimination and entitlement hidden in the shadows of my self-righteousness. Forgive me. Let mercy reign.*

I began to look up and meet the eyes of my fellow weary travelers, imparting dignity. I nodded at them with kindness. I reached out my arms and offered to hold wiggling toddlers. I smiled with understanding at their tired faces, because I understood. I truly understood.

I was now one of them.

For those of you who are keeping track, the heart issues that had risen to the surface (so far) in this crucible were pride, denial, self-righteousness, disdain, and a short-lived but very real contempt for others.

After a few long weeks, we received an offer from the DA. Craig's two charges of assault and DUI should have resulted in a total of four years in jail, which could likely be translated to a one-year sentence with good behavior. Furthermore, our attorney was 95 percent certain the court would approve work release during his sentence, allowing him to attend work and college classes. Either way, jail was a certainty.

The final court date for sentencing was set for the middle of July, just twenty-four days before our daughter's wedding. In a short time he would stand before the judge and officially accept the offer from the DA and go to jail.

Jail.

Definition of jail: *noun* \ jāl\

1. a place of confinement for persons held in lawful custody; specifically: such a place under the jurisdiction of a local government (such as a county) for the confinement of persons awaiting trial or those convicted of minor crimes.

2. a place at which you never, ever, want to see your child held; specifically: the ultimate parenting fail destination.

There is nothing that spells FAILURE as clearly as J-A-I-L-T-I-M-E. It's the worst parenting "F Word" of all, even though it actually begins with a J. All the banners that previously hung over my life were ripped down and replaced with FAILURE with a capital J.

It was the ultimate parenting fail destination.

Our next few months were spent dancing the continued bipolar two-step of planning our daughter's wedding and waiting for the final court appearance. One moment I would be wiping tears of joy as my daughter tried on wedding gowns, and the next wiping tears of sadness as I drove away from a drug-testing lab. Into these spaces I carried the raw emotions of humiliation, worry, and a sense of utter failure heavily and secretly and quietly.

I longed to again worry about the "little" things of life. I wanted to feel anxiety over broken appliances and the check engine light. I welcomed the thought of once again feeling the weight of insignificant things.

I desperately wanted to laugh again. I longed for that beautiful feeling of laughing so hard, with tears spilling out of your eyes, that you silently shake and can't quite catch your breath. Our family was crazy amounts of fall-down funny, and we used to laugh so much.

During this season we took a very long, hard personal inventory of our parenting style. *We should have read more parenting books. We should have read fewer books. We should have asked more questions. We were too hard. We were too lenient. We expected too much. We didn't expect enough. We should have waited to have kids until we were older and wiser.*

All the judging, assuming, accusing words of my Christian parenting world returned to me. I didn't even need the enemy to whisper to me, as I was articulating the judgments in long and complete sentences for him.

It seems as though this season lasted a very long time, but in truth it was only about four months before I finally pulled myself together. And by "pulled myself together" I mean that I allowed the Word of God and the work of the Holy Spirit to redemptively begin to work through all the ugly that had risen to the surface.

Here's the thing about the enemy of our souls: he exists to steal, kill, and destroy. One of his greatest weapons of mass destruction is getting us to agree with a lie. It's not enough that he lies to our hearts, but the pin is pulled on that grenade when he can get us to agree with the lie.

Here's the thing about our situation: it was real. It wasn't a lie. It was the absolute, unbelievable reality of our lives. Our prodigal child's wanderings were about to take us all to a new and unthinkable destination called jail.

The journey of the past four months had been a fiery furnace where the muck and impurities that rose to the surface were *not* useful to the battle but were necessary for me to identify and remove in order to move forward. These four months were only Phase I of the clean sweep needed to clear out my vessel for usefulness.

Remove the dross from the silver,
    and a silversmith can produce a vessel.—PROVERBS 25:4 (NIV)

Thankfully, because of my relationship with Scripture over the course of my life, specifically with my trusted Thompson Chain Reference NIV, I held the source for placing the pins back in the threatening grenades.

Over the years I had meditated on Scripture and even committed some of it to memory. The verses tucked into my heart-file were most certainly meant for such a time as this. The onslaught of mud-mucked emotion and worry and condemnation I was experiencing as I drove from catering appointments with my precious daughter to drug-testing labs with my any-moment-to-be-jailed precious son required a response.

I'm afraid . . . *I sought the LORD, and he answered me;*
he delivered me from all my fears.—PSALM 34:4 (NIV)

One pin returned to the grenade.

I'm helpless . . . *For I am the LORD your God,*
who takes hold of your right hand
and says to you, Do not fear;
I will help you.—ISAIAH 41:13 (NIV)

Another safely disarmed.

I feel hopeless . . . *Guide me in your truth and teach me,*
for you are God my Savior,
and my hope is in you all day long.—PSALM 25:5 (NIV)

I can't see how this is going to work . . . *For we live by faith,*
not by sight.—2 CORINTHIANS 5:7 (NIV)

I deeply resent this place in which we find ourselves . . .
Consider it all joy, my brethren, when you encounter various trials, knowing that the testing of your faith produces endurance. And let endurance have its perfect result, so that you may be perfect and complete, lacking in nothing.
—JAMES 1:2–4 (NASB)

My child is in a pit . . . . . . *who redeems your life from the pit*
and crowns you with love and compassion,—PSALM 103:4 (NIV)

I feel abandoned . . . *Remember the former things of old;*
for I am God, and there is no other;
* I am God, and there is none like me,*
declaring the end from the beginning
* and from ancient times things not yet done,*
saying, "My counsel shall stand,
* and I will accomplish all my purpose."*—ISAIAH 46:9–10 (ESV)

I'm distracted by comparison . . . *Let your eyes look straight*
* ahead;*
fix your gaze directly before you.—PROVERBS 4:25 (NIV)

The battle is too hard . . . *For we do not wrestle against flesh*
and blood, but against the rulers, against the authorities,
against the cosmic powers over this present darkness,
against the spiritual forces of evil in the heavenly places.
—EPHESIANS 6:12 (ESV)

I need a miracle . . . *For the kingdom of God is not a matter of talk*
but of power.—1 CORINTHIANS 4:20 (NIV)

I feel like giving up . . . *Commit everything you do to the LORD.*
Trust Him, and He will help you.—PSALM 37:5 (NLT)

My child is far from his childhood faith . . . *God frees prisoners—*
he gives sight to the blind,
he lifts up the fallen.—PSALM 146:8–9 (MSG)

The way back seems impossible . . . *"The things which are*
impossible with men are possible with God."—LUKE 18:27 (ASV)

Life didn't turn out like I planned . . . *I believe that I shall look*
* upon the goodness of the LORD*
in the land of the living!—PSALM 27:13 (ESV)

I'm unsteady . . . *Let us hold unswervingly to the hope we profess,*
for he who promised is faithful.—HEBREWS 10:23 (NIV)

I'm disoriented ... *The LORD is my Shepherd, I lack nothing.*
He makes me lie down in green pastures,
he leads me beside quiet waters.—PSALM 23:1–2 (NIV)

I trained my child in the Lord, and it didn't work ... *"You know*
with all your heart and soul that not one of all the good
promises the LORD your God gave you has failed."— JOSHUA
23:14 (NIV)

I'm hurting about my child and the choices he's made ...
Be kind and compassionate to one another, forgiving each
other, just as in Christ God forgave you.—EPHESIANS 4:31–32 (NIV)

I've lost my joy ... *Your statutes are my heritage forever;*
they are the joy of my heart.—PSALM 119:111 (NIV)

I can't sleep ... *By day the LORD directs his love,*
at night his song is with me—
a prayer to the God of my life.—PSALM 42:8 (NIV)

I've lost my confidence that this will work out ... *We are the*
true circumcision, who worship in the Spirit of God and
glory in Christ Jesus and put no confidence in the flesh.
—PHILIPPIANS 3:3 (NASB)

I'm heartbroken ... *If your heart is broken, you'll find God*
right there;
if you're kicked in the gut, he'll help you catch your breath.
—PSALM 34:18 (MSG)

Each verse a rescue. One verse at a time. Over and over and over
again. One upon the other until I disarmed all the agreements and
pacts I had made with this "Failure Fallout."

Failure was a revealing fire.

There would be more revealing and refining to come. More impurities would rise to the surface in this hot refinery. I learned to
identify the platform of Scripture from which eventually I would
find solid footing.

Five

DELI COUNTERS
Waiting

I am a major Rocky Balboa fan. It's actually kind of embarrassing. My only wish for my sixteenth birthday was to go to a big theater and watch *Rocky III*, because, after all, *it's the eye of the tiger, it's the thrill of the fight*. I still remember driving across town from Arvada to the Cooper Theatre on Colorado Blvd., which felt like a hundred miles from home, adding to the thrill and adventure.

The Cooper had a ginormous curved screen with a huge, heavy red curtain that slowly pulled back as the lights dimmed. I'll never forget sitting in my plush seat in the cool, air-conditioned space on that hot August day, so cold you could punch a side of beef for training purposes, as the curtain revealed the United Artists logo and the *Rocky III* graphic swept from right to left across Rocky's championship belt. My heart practically burst out of my chest.

I can't actually watch the brutality of real-life boxing, but I never seem to tire of watching the Italian Stallion hand it to Apollo Creed and Clubber Lang. It's no surprise that my child's prodigal journey felt like a brutal boxing match. Each decision felt like a devastating blow. Every court appointment left me bloodied and sprawled on the mat.

While reeling from the painful blows of your wandering child, you will suffer massive hits from the sucker-punches of Doubt and Comparison. Finish it off with side digs of Resentment, and you are sitting in the corner chair of the boxing ring, with Micky pressing some steel thing-y to your eye to reduce the swelling, and you're screaming "Adriaaaan!" from the side of your mouth that still works.

Every mom you see will seem to have the rose-colored stain of joy and order on her cheeks, while you have tender, bloody, swollen gashes of chaos on yours. You become hyper aware of other families that are happy and whole.

I felt as though I had a split personality between court-mandated this-and-that-requirement-with-totally-devastating-results-if-you-let-anything-slip-through-the-crack, while joyfully and genuinely planning a wedding. Add to the personality layers my attempts at managing and maintaining a healthy home environment for three younger children ages ten, thirteen, and fifteen. It left me bloodied and bruised.

All I could see were healthy, whole families everywhere I looked. No trauma. No pain. Health and joy. And wholeness. That's all I could see.

The floodgate of comparison was upon me. For those of you who have never played, the comparison game is brutal. The comparison game with "successful" families is especially crushing when you have a prodigal child, because you are not comparing "stuff" but the most precious gifts God has entrusted you with. The raising of our children is not merely our life's work; it's all about God's valuable, entrusted treasure.

"We were a good family like that one, and now we are not."

It seemed as though everybody else's family was doing great. Nobody was struggling. All their kids were turning out incredible. I tried to push back the curtains of resentment, but they were stuck, as though one of the rings were lodged in a crack along the curtain rod I couldn't see, high above my reach.

While peering into the lives of others, I felt terribly excluded from all the incredible, amazing family returns on their investments.

When I was a little girl, I endured some fairly severe childhood asthma. What could now be treated with a rescue inhaler or nebulizer treatment at home had meant hospitalization and a few days under an oxygen tent for me if I came into contact with a full-of-the-devil cat or some other trigger. *Please forgive me, cat owners. I'm sure your cat is super lovely and not at all full of the devil.* One vivid memory was of my grandparents fortieth wedding anniversary celebration.

I was in the hospital, stuck in an oxygen tent, while the rest of my family celebrated somewhere outside the hospital walls. When they returned to my tent, I'll never forget my Grandma and Grandpa Torrez, wearing carnations on their lapels from the celebration, reaching under the oxygen tent to tenderly love me with their precious familiar hands and sneak me a few bites of their anniversary cake.

I was so sad to have missed out on the celebration, and as I peered out of the plastic tent walls I felt sorry for myself. I was so sad to be here while they were there. Because of my self-pity, I missed out on the sweet joy right there in the hospital room with me. Two loving grandparents who drove themselves to the hospital after their glorious celebration to visit their sick granddaughter. This should have filled my little heart with joy, but I was distracted by the thing I had been denied.

I would never describe myself as competitive. I actually have a violent dislike for competitive stuff. But here was my whole life's work of mothering, and I had come up short. Terribly short. I didn't care about the title Supermom, but I desperately tried to be a good one. I held supermoms in the highest esteem, as though I were a bystander, not actually participating in the same competition.

Instead of not caring what people thought, I realized I cared far too much.

I knew I needed to fix my eyes on Jesus. I knew that now was not the time for the enemy's distractions, comparisons, or competition.

I knew better. They are not useful in the battle in which I needed to fully engage.

In this waiting season, which revealed the new players called Comparison, Worry, and Resentment (this "Phase II"), I pushed hard against the blows of Despair. I was trying so hard to fight but found myself in the grip of a profound exhaustion. With every day I grew more and more dispirited, as the journey almost swallowed me whole. I reminded myself that "God works in our waiting," but I didn't quite know how long I could wait. I tried to believe that Jesus can make waters run back upstream, but the waters just continued to rush downward.

I lost my eyelashes. I didn't even know that was a thing. My eyelashes were literally wiped off my eyelids. Googling the phrase "how to regrow eyelashes" became a small, distracting pastime in the middle of the storm.

I desperately determined that my son's siblings would not suffer neglect as I clung to the wreckage of our family dynamic. I was filled with a determination to preserve my family while gripped with a raw anxiety bred of worry and failure. I was going through the motions, one minute calm and composed and the next hysterical and weepy, hiding in the bathroom.

Bathrooms can get freakishly clean when moms use them to hide.

More than once, while I was waiting for roast beef at the deli counter, tears would rush down my cheeks. I've never been blessed with the ability to cry discreetly. My nose turns bright red before the first tear falls, like a blaring, blinking sign to all humanity. As though I'm a truck in reverse, my nose acts as a back-up beeper. At least the red nose was a distraction from the three-solitary-eyelash situation.

As I was a repeat offender, the deli worker knew me well and would simply hand me a thin square of unwaxed deli paper meant for samples for use as a tissue before handing me my order. "Here's a little paper for your nose, and here's your 1.5 pounds of thin sliced roast beef, ma'am."

This fiery trial of waiting for jail was of such epic proportions it threatened to undo my trust in God's goodness. It hijacked my peace. It hid my joy. It picked the lock on the safety of my heart with a tiny, menacing bobby pin. It dumped water on the fiery coals of my love for my calling as a mother.

Beloved, do not be surprised at the fiery trial when it comes upon you to test you, as though something strange were happening to you. But rejoice insofar as you share Christ's sufferings, that you may also rejoice and be glad when his glory is revealed.—1 PETER 4:12–13 (ESV)

Jesus was inviting me to enter joy and gladness. During the most bitter, heart-shattering, grueling journey of my life. His glory was about to be revealed. *How was that even possible?*

Instead of walking away from these hard verses, I decided to walk all the way into them. I didn't fully understand them. *How could this situation possibly reveal His glory?*

My child was about to step through a threshold that threatened his already broken spiritual condition and his entire future. He remained distant, unchanged, and seemingly unaware of the severity of our situation. He felt far away as we were marching toward a frightening destination.

I learned to depend on Scripture, not merely for dismantling the enemy's strategies but for my very survival. For my very living and breathing. It was my only source. Only through the reality of Scripture and the power of the Holy Spirit could I truly find hope in the midst of this situation.

I finally gave in to the blows. I let my gloves and arms dangle helplessly at the sides of my body and gave myself fully to the hard work. This ridiculous battle with Comparison was getting me nowhere. Worry over the unknown, impending jail experience and how it would impact our son's life was a dead end. Resentment was even worse. They led me down paths of doubt and distrust. I closed the door on these unfaithful, distracting sparring partners.

Six

PSALMS
Crying Out

Before this prodigal season my entire book of Psalms was already highlighted. Pale yellow, pink, and blue highlights marked every page. Every "Hear, O LORD, and answer me, for I am poor and needy" was underlined and circled. Asterisks and little hearts lined the margins.

For the first time, in this crazy brutal battle for my son, I understood the heart of the psalmists.

This prodigal season was a suffering season. It was a revealing season of identifying fear, pride, isolation, denial, comparison, worry, and resentment. It was an intimidating season in which our son's future was in the balance.

It was a heartbreaking season.

The season seemed to move in slow motion, and it proved to be the testing ground for my entire life's system of beliefs and convictions. Beyond revealing my own heart condition, I was crying out for the rescue of my son. The combination of revealing and crying out led me to fully recognize my deep awareness of my need for God at every moment.

I found more of God in the depths of my suffering.

Finally, intentionally and purposefully, I allowed the suffering season to strengthen and purify my faith in God's promises. I had always *believed* that only Jesus could offer inexpressible joy in the most heartbreaking and excruciating circumstances, but now I *knew* it. The promise of His nearness was the rescue I so desperately needed.

The shame of my prideful, fearful, self-focused, competitive, and worried heart revealed in Phases I and II desperately needed reversal. My son needed rescuing.

I now understood that God promised He would *be with me* through the suffering, which is the greatest promise of all. His presence. He offered unique provision in the desolation.

This suffering season became an invitation to deeper maturity. It led me to the waters of deeper compassion. It rounded the bend to deeper humility. It increased my awareness of my absolute need for God and released my death grip on self. I had always known I needed him—I had even memorized songs that described my need for Him—but oh, how I needed Him now. The reducing work of this season made way for a deep work of the Spirit.

> *Deep calls to deep*
> *in the roar of your waterfalls;*
> *all your waves and breakers*
> *have swept over me.*—PSALM 42:7 (NIV)

The hot fire of refinement left me withered, as though I were standing in the middle of a hot, dry field, unprotected, vulnerable, and alone. Each day left me parched and in need of the streams, rain, and rivers found only in the waterfall of His Presence.

> *He shall be like a tree*
> *Planted by the rivers of water,*
> *That brings forth its fruit in its season,*
> *Whose leaf also shall not wither;*
> *And whatever he does shall prosper.*—PSALM 1:3 (NKJV)

For he shall be like a tree planted by the waters,
Which spreads out its roots by the river,
And will not fear when heat comes;
But its leaf will be green,
And will not be anxious in the year of drought,
Nor will cease from yielding fruit.—JEREMIAH 17:8 (NKJV)

This brutal, stunning, and purposefully parched ground redemptively pushed my faith forward. God used this dry season to pull my self-righteous, sedentary faith into action. He was introducing Himself to me in a deeper way. He began revealing Himself and renewing my confidence in His character.

I had been crying out to the Lord this entire time, but now I was literally *crying out to the Lord.*

The psalms gave voice to my cries and language to my prayers.

The psalmists lifted their voice to God with cries for help. They were brutally honest about their struggle. They felt God's absence, and they felt God's presence. They felt them both at the same time. Their admitted their soul's thirst and worked through their pain to a resolution of praise.

I now understood the heart of the psalmists.

When our children were little, we had created prayer notebooks for them, and we journaled through our prayers each evening. We used the traditional outline of A.C.T.S. = Adoration, Confession, Thanksgiving, and Supplication. We jotted down little moments of thanksgiving in their notebooks to remind our kids that God was so good to us. Altars of remembrance. Moments like: "When Amanda was playing on the computer and she accidentally swallowed a quarter and it got stuck in her throat, Jesus helped her. That was scary, but Jesus rescued her." These moments helped build our kids' faith.

This new, desperate praying through the book of Psalms worked the same way for me. I built new altars of remembrance. I confessed new revelations of unbelief. I built a new, deeper level of faith.

Working through the psalms reoriented me by giving me the clarity of a new perspective of gratitude *while* enabling me to be very honest about the struggle. It renewed my awe. It increased my faith. It moved me from a mere exchange of desperate information to a genuine, active conversation with God. It provided a safe haven for my heart. Every emotion I tried to stuff down was described in the psalms.

Equipped as I was with new eyes, this book showed me how to pray with new understanding of His character and will. One day He was my Shepherd, the next day my King. His character unfolded in rich, new Technicolor, and in rich language. I had read these prayer songs before, but never through this heart filter. It helped me pray with directness, instead of praying what I thought would please God. It articulated my response to God.

It also made way for me to *listen* to God.

It moved me beyond merely praying to *get* something—not that I didn't really need something—to experiencing His presence, which far outweighed any getting I could ask for. It loosened my death-grip on the good things I clung to for happiness. My immersion in the psalms saturated my prayer life with His presence and reminded me of my grandparents' morning prayer routine with open Bibles.

Ultimately, the psalms led my dry heart to the work of the cross, like a burdened beast to water. I let the water flow. The cross bids us to believe that He is for us and not against us. He sees us. He knows us. We are His beloved.

> *You have searched me, LORD,*
> *   and you know me.*
> *You know when I sit and when I rise;*
> *   you perceive my thoughts from afar.*
> *You discern my going out and my lying down;*
> *   you are familiar with all my ways.*
> *Before a word is on my tongue*
> *   you, LORD, know it completely.*
> *You hem me in behind and before,*
> *   and you lay your hand upon me.*
> *Such knowledge is too wonderful for me,*
> *   too lofty for me to attain.*

Where can I go from your Spirit?
Where can I flee from your presence?
If I go up to the heavens, you are there;
if I make my bed in the depths, you are there.
If I rise on the wings of the dawn,
if I settle on the far side of the sea,
even there your hand will guide me,
your right hand will hold me fast.
If I say "Surely the darkness will hide me
and the light become night around me,"
even the darkness will not be dark to you;
the night will shine like the day,
for darkness is as light to you.

For you created my inmost being;
you knit me together in my mother's womb.
I praise you because I am fearfully and wonderfully made;
your works are wonderful,
I know that full well.
My frame was not hidden from you
when I was made in the secret place,
when I was woven together in the depths of the earth.
Your eyes saw my unformed body;
all the days ordained for me were written in your book
before one of them came to be.
How precious to me are your thoughts, God!
How vast is the sum of them!
Were I to count them,
they would outnumber the grains of sand—
when I awake, I am still with you.—Psalm 139:1–18 (NIV)

Through this psalm watering, I began to refresh others again. My walking rhythm synced with the Spirit's. My overreacting self was calmed and steadied. I understood that He was providing everything I needed for each day.

Instead of striving for my son, I could now serve him with

confidence. Instead of reacting with hurt, I could respond with compassion. Instead of viewing other happy families with resentment, I could again rejoice with them.

The anchor for my soul in the midst of this epic boxing match is the greater knowledge of the goodness and grace of God at work in my life. The psalms reminded me that the God who hung the stars sees me, sees my circumstance, and sees my son. In the midst of the immensity of the universe, and in the midst of this desperate and confusing season, I remembered that He cares for me, and that He cares for my son.

Seven

LUKE 15
Lost Things

As with the psalms, I also became best friends with Luke 15. Together with my husband, Craig, we made it our reference point for moving forward. It showed us how to pursue our son in this lost season.

I couldn't get enough. I read the chapter over and over and over. I saw the God of Luke through a new, previously undiscovered Instagram filter. I learned a new angle, the driving heartbeat of this God I've loved my whole life: He searches for and finds lost things.

Some aspects of the will of God are difficult to discern, but this one was obvious: He seeks and saves the lost. He *loves* my prodigal child, *pursues* him, and *wants* him. He is the God who seeks and saves.

He is *all* about lost things.

First of all, let me say that these parables found in Luke 15 are about ALL of us. *All* of us have sinned and rebelled against an extravagant, loving heavenly Father. Jesus came to seek and save the lost. That's us. Each one of us. We are *all* fallen, sinful, and rebellious. All of us are prodigal sons and daughters, lost coins and lost sheep, found by a relentlessly loving Father.

The beautiful, stunning themes in this trio of parables became a lifeline for me. Each parable drives the same point home, while the third one sheds an extra measure of beautiful light on the nature of the Father and his two sons. He knew we needed the subplot of the resentful elder brother as a dig at the hypocritical Pharisees and scribes whose grumblings prompted the parables in the first place.

Each parable drives home God's open-armed stance toward lost sinners, and the outpouring of joy and gladness he lavishes on them. Each describes the loss of a seemingly replaceable possession, hardly worth the effort: a sheep, a coin, a son. The shepherd had ninety-nine unlost sheep, for goodness sake; the woman had nine other coins in safekeeping; and the Father, although heartsick over the loss of his son, was not without another son. The losing of something of little or no value is an inconvenience but not a life-altering blow. The losing of something of great value is a totally different story. The sheep, coin, and son were in reality of *immense* value.

These parables describe the shepherd, the woman, and the father, respectively, descending from their rightful safe position to the hard, dirty, and undignified work while looking for their valuable lost possession.

Now the tax collectors and sinners were all drawing near to him. And the Pharisees and the scribes grumbled, saying, "This man receives sinners and eats with them."

So he told them this parable: "What man of you, having a hundred sheep, if he has lost one of them, does not leave the ninety-nine in the open country, and go after the one that is lost, until he finds it? And when he has found it, he lays it on his shoulders, rejoicing. And when he comes home, he calls together his friends and his neighbors, saying to them, 'Rejoice with me, for I have found my sheep that was lost.' Just so, I tell you, there will be more joy in heaven over one sinner who repents than over ninety-nine righteous persons who need no repentance."—Luke 15:1–7 (ESV)

"Or what woman, having ten silver coins, if she loses one coin, does not light a lamp and sweep the house and seek carefully until she finds it? And when she has found it, she calls together her friends and neighbors, saying, 'Rejoice with me, for I have found the coin that I had lost!' Just so, I tell you, there is joy before the angels of God over one sinner who repents."—LUKE 15:8–10 (ESV)

In the first parable Jesus used the very familiar cultural image of sheep and a shepherd. His audience got it. All within earshot would have understood immediately the imagery and context. They knew sheep. All they would have needed to do for reference was peek around the corner toward the nearest hillside to view a shepherd tending his flock. The shepherd has one hundred valuable sheep and loses one.

The lost sheep would have likely been in danger, would soon have died if left to wander by itself in the wilderness. Anyone who knows Psalm 23 understands the basics of a shepherd's job, which is to lead his flocks *to* food and water and *away* from predators. Even a thin understanding of Scripture informs our Western minds on the scope and sequence of Shepherding 101.

I confess that my limited understanding of shepherding came from my years as a children's church choir director. In preparation for one of my many Christmas musicals, I created flocks of paper mâché "sheep" in my dining room, fleecing them with cotton balls, hooving them with blackened dixie cups, and hot-gluing them to the bottom of my "shepherd staffs" as portable props for my little boy shepherds to carry on and off stage.

Actual shepherds were amazing.

They would lead their flocks to cracks in the rock and caves to protect their charges from the elements. They led their sheep toward food and water. They fought off lions and bears and wolves. Basically, the lost sheep was doomed without the safekeeping of the shepherd.

**Our son Craig's name means
"someone who dwells in the crack of the rock."
Coincidence? I think not.**

Actual shepherds were committed and compassionate. It was the shepherd's understanding, duty, and compassion that led him to leave the ninety-nine (dare I say "well-behaved"?) sheep and climb through Lord only knows what landscape to retrieve his filthy lost sheep and "lay it on his shoulders rejoicing" as he carried the dirty, mud-encrusted creature home. The passage doesn't say "and lo, he struck him with his staff in great anger" when he found it. He lifted it up and carried the filthy animal with great joy.

In the second parable, the woman had ten valuable coins and lost one.

It seems a small thing to lose one-tenth of her silver coins, but there was nothing small about her loss. She was relentless. She turned her house upside down, searching the darkness of each dirty corner with an oil lamp. She was determined and didn't miss an inch. She left nothing unturned. She was persistent. *There is no actual way to arrive at victory without persistence.*

She was persistent.

When she found the lost coin, she could have easily slipped it into her pocket and gone about her business with a sense of relief. No one would have known. Instead, she joyfully gathered her friends for a dance party. The finding was cause for rejoicing. Earthly rejoicing and heavenly rejoicing.

In each of these two stories, we found ourselves. Dirty and heat-exhausted, wrestling a mud-crusted lost sheep out of a gnarled tree, like the shepherd. Desperately holding a lamp and a broom, kicking up dust in search of our lost coin, like the woman.

> **When these parables become living,**
> **breathing examples of your life,**
> **they bring new life and hope to your journey.**

The third parable was where I found the most beautiful and nuanced truths. I was held together by every single word. I feasted on its outer layer and middle sections and dug into the secret new undertones of the veiled layers.

And he said, "There was a man who had two sons. And the younger of them said to his father, 'Father, give me the share of property that is coming to me.' And he divided his property between them. Not many days later, the younger son gathered all he had and took a journey into a far country, and there he squandered his property in reckless living. And when he had spent everything, a severe famine arose in that country, and he began to be in need. So he went and hired himself out to one of the citizens of that country, who sent him into his fields to feed pigs. And he was longing to be fed with the pods that the pigs ate, and no one gave him anything.

"But when he came to himself, he said, 'How many of my father's hired servants have more than enough bread, but I perish here with hunger! I will arise and go to my father, and I will say to him, "Father, I have sinned against heaven and before you. I am no longer worthy to be called your son. Treat me as one of your hired servants."' And he arose and came to his father. But while he was still a long way off, his father saw him and felt compassion, and ran and embraced him and kissed him. And the son said to him, 'Father, I have sinned against heaven and before you. I am no longer worthy to be called your son.' But the father said to his servants, 'Bring quickly the best robe, and put it on him, and put a ring on his hand, and shoes on his feet. And bring the fattened calf and kill it, and let us eat and celebrate. For this my son was dead, and is alive again; he was lost, and is found.' And they began to celebrate.

"Now his older son was in the field, and as he came and drew near to the house, he heard music and dancing. And he called one of the servants and asked what these things meant. And he said to him, 'Your brother has come, and your father has killed the fattened calf, because he has received him back safe and sound.' But he was angry and refused to go in. His father came out and entreated him, but he answered his father, 'Look, these many years I have served you, and I never disobeyed your command, yet you never gave me a young goat, that I might *celebrate with my friends. But when this son of yours came, who has devoured your property with prostitutes, you killed the fattened calf for him!' And he said to him, 'Son, you are always with me, and all that is mine is yours. It was fitting to celebrate and be glad, for this your brother was dead, and is alive; he was lost, and is found.'"*—LUKE 15:11–32 (ESV)

The depth of the son's recklessness and wastefulness is crazy amounts of painful when it's actually happening to you. The son's attitude toward his father creates a seismic crack in your heart. It's so very personal. The seeming disregard for the wealth and love and legacy is heart-rending.

Don't even get me started on the spirit of the elder brother and how it pierced my heart. His language was all "I don't deserve," "What about me?" and "How dare you let this happen," which describes my entire chapter on denial. Hello, pierced heart.

The prodigal son was clearly miserable and wanted what he wanted as he expressed total and utter disregard for his father. *Check.* His actions went beyond dishonor. *Check.* He wanted more independence, and he wasted his present and future inheritance to finance his reckless journey and ultimate meltdown. *Check.* He was blinded by "now." *Check.* He was looking for pleasure. *Check.* He squandered his spiritual inheritance and the blessing of his father. *Check.* He never counted the cost. *Check.* He squandered every opportunity and blessing his father extended. *Check.*

He was pulled down into a free fall and found himself facedown in the mud. He experienced a meltdown of epic proportions. His recklessness did not pay off. He was destitute, friendless, and starving. His entire life was lying in ruins. He ended up powerless and enslaved. Small. Broken. Swineherding. He descended so low he found himself living in the filth of pigs.

For the wages of sin is death, but the free gift of God is eternal life in Christ Jesus our Lord.—ROMANS 6:23 (ESV)

Sin-sickness, left untreated, is irrational and shortsighted.

The son's actions were so striking and so utterly relatable.

Some of us are not able to stand at a distance from this parable and learn its lessons in a tidy, controlled Bible study format. Some of us have lived it. The slop from the pigpen has entered the doors of our home. Sin contaminates all it touches, and it never delivers what it promises. It leaves a film on every family gathering, conversation, and holiday.

In the prodigal son's story, I clung to a few beautiful things I had never noticed before: "he gathered all he had and took a journey into a far country." He gathered all he had. My son gathered *all* he had and took it with him. My wandering son took a lifetime of loving Jesus with him to a far country. His experience with Jesus and the Holy Spirit was *with him* on this journey. He didn't leave it at home. He gathered *all he had.*

Here's another thing I had never before noticed: when the son came to his senses, the first thing he remembered was his father. He remembered. His thoughts turned his heart homeward. He had experienced the kindness and generosity of his father his entire life, and they remained with him. He remembered that his father's servants always had "more than enough bread."

> **I tuned my heart to the lead character,**
> **this extravagant parent, who showed me**
> **the way to love my son.**

The love of this father. This father who extended undeserved grace upon grace. This father whose actual wealth was measured in outrageous amounts of tender love and compassion. He was patient, loving, and generous. His love was profound. He generously and quickly restored his son. Plain and simple. The father demonstrated mercy. He endured the pain of his son's rejection. He swatted public rejection off his shoulder like a pesky fly.

The father's love for both of his children was profound. He was full of longsuffering and forbearance toward *both* sons. Later, in the unresolved story of his other shameful and ungrateful son, we see that he extended the very same invitations of love and relationship.

All the disgust the father could have poured out on his sons was absorbed in the death of Jesus on the cross.

Here's another thing I clung to: "while he was still a long way off, his father saw him and felt compassion, and ran and embraced him and kissed him." This meant that the father wasn't stuck in bed hiding under the covers. He didn't isolate himself, as I had, and miss out on the opportunity coming over the hill. He was out in public, on his porch, in plain view, gazing so hard at the horizon that he saw his son *while he was a long way off*. Daily heartbroken, but hopeful in looking.

Some of us know the desire to pull the blinds, remove ourselves, isolate ourselves, and hide. The father's public porch waiting bolstered me out of bed. He watched. He waited. He expected. He bore the shame. Day after heartbreaking day. I could do the same.

He wasn't disgusted with his son. He didn't hold his son in contempt and condescension. He didn't view his son as "too morally compromised" to look for. Quite the opposite. His son was of great value to him.

The whole story hinged on the father's response. HE was the one who made full reconciliation available. He was eager to restore relationship. He didn't make the son wait outside the city gates, bearing the community's dishonor by himself. The community no doubt held the son in profound contempt. The father wasn't granting a small measure of mercy and a repayment schedule—he was eager to forgive. Freely and completely. There was nothing small about his response.

He ran.

Before the son spoke one word of his prepared speech, forgiveness was extended. That father hitched up his robe, showed his bare dad legs, and took off in a full-on sprint. He humbled himself and humiliated himself by running. This was the loudest restoring to sonship his community had ever seen. Not only did he love his son, but he took on shame and willingly wiped his dirty slate clean. He held nothing back to restore his son. He was reckless with his forgiveness. Honor upon honor after receiving dishonor upon dishonor. *What?!*

The best of all he had belonged to his son. Shoes. Robe. Ring. Fatted Calf. Feast. Dancing. Rejoicing. Like other examples of biblical forgiveness, it was lavish. Otherworldly. Undignified. Extraordinary and over the top.

Somehow, with the grace of God and the power of the Holy Spirit, we needed to move forward with the heart of the shepherd, the woman who had lost her coin, and the prodigal's father. They couldn't remain high and above it all. There was no distancing themselves in safety. They stooped down and rolled up their sleeves in relentless pursuit.

In the early days of our marriage, Craig and I couldn't get enough of our Benny Hester cassette tape, featuring the song "When God Ran." Someday, if I ever meet Benny Hester, I'm going to give him the biggest hug for this song. It will be a strange superfangirl moment, but I'm willing to live with that. Some of you might know the song, and you're singing the tune right now. For those who don't, here are the lyrics. Find the cassette. Buy it. Play it. Play it again. You're welcome.

WHEN GOD RAN

written by Benny Ray Hester, John Parenti

Copyright © Warner/Chappell Music, Inc. Universal Music Publishing Group

Almighty God
The Great I Am
Immovable Rock,
Omnipotent powerful
Awesome Lord
Victorious Warrior
Commanding King of Kings
Mighty Conquerer

And the only time
The only time I ever saw Him run

Was when He ran to me
Took me in His arms, held my head to His chest
Said "My son's come home again"
Lifted my face, wiped the tears from my eyes

With forgiveness in his voice
He said, "Son, do you know I still love you?"

It caught me by surprise when God ran.

The day I left home
I knew I'd broken His heart
I wondered then
If things could ever be the same
Then one night
I remembered His love for me
And down that dusty road
Ahead I could see

It's the only time
The only time I ever saw Him run

When He ran to me
Took me in His arms, held my head to His chest
Said "My son's come home again"
Lifted my face, wiped the tears from my eyes

With forgiveness in his voice
He said, "Son, do you know I still love you?"

It caught me by surprise
It brought me to my knees
When God ran

I saw Him run to me
And then I ran to Him

Holy One, Righteous Judge
He turned my way
Now I know He's been waiting
For this day

And then He ran to me
Took me in His arms, held my head to His chest
Said "My son's come home again"
Lifted my face, wiped the tears from my eyes

With forgiveness in his voice
He said, Son! He said Son! My Son!
Do you know I still love you?
Do you know I still love you?
Oh He ran to me

When God ran

Eight

ROCK BOTTOM
Handcuffed

*You don't really know Jesus is all you need
until Jesus is all you have.*—Tim Keller

Amidst wedding showers and flowers and preparations, Craig Jr.'s final court date arrived.

I fully intended to go into the courtroom with my husband and son that day. We dressed up. I pressed a shirt for my son, laid out a tie for him, and refreshed the creases on his dress pants, as was my new custom for our court appearances. We drove together, with me sitting in the back of the car, reaching forward and gently touching his shoulder as we made our way down the interstate.

When we pulled into the parking lot, though, my legs wouldn't work, even though I willed them to walk. It wasn't a long and drawn-out dramatic scene; I simply couldn't walk. Quickly, I hugged him and kissed his face and told him I loved him so much and waited in the car while I watched the two of them, clean-cut handsome as ever father and son, walk into the county court building.

Our son was quiet. Serious, respectful, and attentive. He was remorseful without a hint of arrogance. He was strong and he was brave.

Craig promised to give me a blow-by-blow via texts as I lay down in the backseat of the car, praying for a miraculous last-minute change of mind and mercy from the court. They waited, father and son, in the courtroom for what seemed like a long time, witnessing defendant after defendant sentenced, handcuffed, and led away.

Finally, it was our son's turn. He stood in front of the judge and officially accepted the plea bargain offered by the DA a few short months earlier. He answered a few questions indicating that he understood the sentence, and that was it.

Just like that.

Our son quickly handed his tie, belt, and cell phone to his dad and proceeded past the little wooden gate that separates the judge from the defendants to a waiting deputy to be handcuffed. They led him out a door behind the judge.

Just like that.

In that moment my husband was struck with all the overwhelming emotions life could possibly stuff into a single human body. A few moments ago, he was sitting next to our precious son, and now he was returning to our car alone. With sad and defeated hands he carried our son's wallet, belt, tie, and cell phone out to the too-bright parking lot in the too-alive outside world.

Just like that.

He sat in the driver's seat, held on to the steering wheel, and together we sat in complete silence. We had just left our son in jail. Our precious, beloved son.

Deafening amounts of silence were followed by acute tunnel vision. We slipped into a surreal suspended heaviness. The earth was a magnet, and our bodies were made entirely of iron. At the same time, I felt strangely untethered, as though gravity had lost its hold. Heavy and weightless at the same time.

All the prayer in the world wouldn't change the fact that we were driving away with his wallet, belt, tie, and cell phone. I held them with precious awe and horror. My throat felt choked, and I couldn't form words. I was surprised to discover that my dried up, iron-filled body still had the moisture to produce tears, and I let them fall on the items held in my hands.

When we returned home, we sat in our car and cried. Exhausted, sad tears.

We made our way to the kitchen and realized we were all squarely flattened against the lowest level of Rock Bottom. Our son in jail and the rest of us sitting in our kitchen. This was it. Bottom level. The broken pieces of our hearts were split and broken. Spilled out.

He needed us, and we couldn't follow him past the wooden gate to wherever they took him.

He needed a toothbrush. And shampoo.

His sentence was set at twenty-four months and could be reduced to twelve months with good behavior. We had to wait forty-eight long hours to hear confirmation of his approval for the work release program, which meant that he would be officially released each morning, enabling him to work at his uncle's landscaping company during the day and attend college classes in the evening before returning to the county jail to sleep and begin again the next day.

He spent the first very traumatic twenty-four hours in a cell by himself, without any human interaction. On day three he was accepted into the work release program and was allowed to come home for one hour to gather clothes for work and school, a toothbrush, and a few other personal items.

**From this moment forward, my pain
turned into the most laser-focused mothering
I have ever done.**

I utterly hurled my whole being into the most basic functions I knew: prayer, Scripture, and serving my family with every fiber of my being—including our son, who needed us now more than ever before, and our daughter, who was getting married in twenty-four days. There was room for nothing else.

I hid myself in the Word.

I could waste no more time bemoaning the injustice of it all. No more shaking my fists at the "unfixable situation" we found ourselves in. More than ever, my thoughts needed the governing of His truth.

Once I had exhausted my voice with all the moaning over my unworthiness, I needed to focus on His great worth. Once I confessed my inability, I needed to focus on His great ability. Once I was drained of my questions, I needed to focus on the One who is the answer.

I needed to point my heart fully to the truth of Jesus, and Jesus alone. I woke and slept with the Word of God pressed to my heart-broken chest. I wrestled with my life's understanding of biblical doctrine, and the nature of His promises. I tuned my broken heart to the faithful comfort of the psalms.

It was time to live out Luke 15.

The words of Scripture held life for me as never before. They were no longer words to be "used" or "memorized" or "applied" like a handbook. They were my actual lifeline.

They healed me, restored my faith, and renewed my hope like a cold glass of water on a sun-torched day.

I recognized that biblical authority didn't rest in the horrible reality of my rock-bottom location but in the reality of God himself. Like a hungry beggar, I drew out the deep meaning of biblical texts. The Word prevented me from falling into complete despair as it focused my heart and mind upon the truth of God's nature and His unchangeable character.

I didn't stay in the refreshing waters of easy, soft, and fluffy Scriptures. I read every single word. I allowed it to scrape to the bottom of my depleted being. I welcomed its hard work. I allowed it to expose me and warn me of the sinful nature of my heart. I allowed it to challenge the things I felt comfortable agreeing with.

I invited the Spirit of God to shape and reshape my convictions. I affirmed and re-affirmed my lifelong confidence in the inspiration and authority of the words I was reading. I allowed the language of Scripture, particularly the psalms, to speak for my broken heart. I allowed His Word to be living and active in my every defeated thought.

I invited His Word to shape me and recreate me. I allowed His

Word to penetrate the silent spiritual apathy that had snuck in during the painful year that led to this point. I welcomed the recalibration of my heart.

I allowed the Word to wake me up to the indifferent corners of my heart. I allowed the Word to tear down my defenses and pride. I allowed it to rewire my opinion of myself—both my prideful, self-righteousness opinions and my low ones. I allowed it to transform my thinking.

**My low point made way for a more profound,
desperate engagement of my heart.**

Read the Word. Speak the Word. Write the Word. Pray the Word. Rehearse the Word. Read it again.

I allowed the Word to bear its full weight on me. The places I had felt were rooted in humility were replaced with true humility. I allowed the Word to increase my understanding of my limitations and embraced my awe at His limitless presence.

His work in my life allowed me to press into the future God intended for my family, while my season of fearful worry threatened to forfeit its possibility.

I allowed it to confirm my confidence in His character, His grace, and His deep, deep commitment to us, His creations.

I allowed it to fully expose my disordered heart. By the grace and goodness of God, I allowed it to break habits and attitudes, including the most natural of all belonging to committed Christian parents: self-reliance and self-righteousness. It wrecked my lazy, "mature" Christian attitudes of "having arrived" and my "knowing-it-all-ness."

I reminded myself that God is absolutely faithful to His promises. I reminded myself that I was not abandoned. My son was not abandoned. God still had an amazing future for me, my family, and my children, which included my now jailed prodigal child.

Though the fig tree should not blossom,
nor fruit be on the vines,

the produce of the olive fail
and the fields yield no food,
the flock be cut off from the fold
and there be no herd in the stalls,
yet I will rejoice in the LORD;
I will take joy in the God of my salvation.
God, the LORD, is my strength;
he makes my feet like the deer's;
he makes me tread on my high places.—HABAKKUK 3:17–19 (ESV)

It was not the time to give up. This was not the moment to throw in the towel. *Pick up that towel, wipe your tears, and stand up. Stay the course. Be faithful. Be fruitful. He can and will work all things for your good and for His great glory.*

When there is defeat, Jesus is not defeated. It's never too late for a miracle.

Lord, I choose to believe you. I choose to praise you. I choose to lift you up over this situation. Addiction will not take hold of my son. Depression will not take hold of my son. Drug abuse will not take hold of my son. Despair will not take hold of my son. Hopelessness will not take hold of my son. Jail will not crush my son. His story is not over.

I was committed to unleash God's power over his life.

I entered into the living, breathing, revealing action of His Word and participated in it. I prayed in the Holy Spirit as never before, and I prayed into the Word and over my children in a new way.

Incrementally, day by day, these verses anchored me:

All your children shall be taught by the LORD,
and great shall be the peace of your children.
—ISAIAH 54:13 (ESV)

The children of your servants shall dwell secure;
their offspring shall be established before you.
—PSALM 102:28 (ESV)

Praise the LORD!

Blessed is the man who fears the LORD,
who greatly delights in his commandments!
His offspring will be mighty in the land;
the generation of the upright will be blessed.—PSALM 112:1–2 (ESV)

For I will pour water on the thirsty land,
and streams on the dry ground;
I will pour my Spirit on your offspring,
and my blessing on your descendants.
They shall spring up among the grass
like willows by flowing streams.—ISAIAH 44:3–4 (ESV)

The righteous who walks in his integrity—
blessed are his children after him.—PROVERBS 20:7 (ESV)

"Therefore you shall keep his statutes and his commandments, which I command you today, that it may go well with you and with your children after you."—DEUTERONOMY 4:40 (ESV)

And they said, "Believe in the Lord Jesus, and you will be saved, you and your household."—Acts 16:31 (ESV)

"I will contend with those who contend with you, and I will save your children."—Isaiah 49:25 (ESV)

Thus says the LORD:

"Refrain your voice from weeping,
And your eyes from tears;
For your work [the raising of your children] shall be rewarded,
says the LORD,

And they shall come back from the land of the enemy.
There is hope in your future, says the LORD,
That your children shall come back to their own border."
—JEREMIAH 31:16–17 (NKJV)

*"And He will love you and bless you and multiply you; He will also bless the fruit of your womb."—*DEUTERONOMY 7:13 (NKJV)

*Behold, children are a heritage from the LORD.—*PSALM 127:3 (NKJV)

In addition to the building of my faith and the revealing of my heart's condition, praying into the Word and over my jailed son and the rest of my children led me back to the waters of gratitude.

There was so much to be grateful for.

Gratitude fortifies respect. Gratitude refocuses our attention. It reveals our character and exposes outdated lies and misunderstandings. It reminds us and prunes us. It brings gladness. Like the old toe-tapping chorus *"I will enter his gates with thanksgiving in my heart/ I will enter his courts with praise/ I will say this is the day that the Lord has made/ I will rejoice for he has made me glad."*

Gratitude fuels gladness. The more gratitude, the more gladness. Just like the song. When my heart began to rehearse gratitude, I remembered abundant life.

*"The thief comes only to steal and kill and destroy. I came that they may have life and have it abundantly."—*JOHN 10:10 (ESV)

Through this jail experience Jesus was leading me back to the deepest life possible, the richest, fullest life imaginable.

You make known to me the path of life;
in your presence there is fullness of joy;
at your right hand are pleasures forevermore.
—PSALM 16:11 (ESV)

My gratitude was allowing me to behold His glory again. The magnitude of the grace and mercy of this God I've known since childhood. His faithfulness in my entire life's story. The God who hung the stars never stopped caring for me. He was wooing me back into the abundant way of living in the midst of the most difficult, flattening battle of my life.

In addition to building up my gratitude muscle, it intensified my worship.

I was invited into something deeper in worship.

Let the word of Christ dwell in you richly, teaching and admonishing one another in all wisdom, singing psalms and hymns and spiritual songs, with thankfulness in your hearts to God.
—COLOSSIANS 3:16 (ESV)

Worship built me and strengthened me for the trial I was enduring. I don't know how it works, but worship is a weapon. It activates the very presence of God and changes us.

So here I was, three weeks away from my daughter's wedding. I was now driving my son from jail to work and from work to college every single day, attending to last-minute wedding details, caring for my three younger children, and hiding myself in the Word and in worship at every single moment in between.

In the midst of this deep, excruciating cleansing, I was not yet ready for public viewing. I was hidden in the Lord but fenced off from others. We were three weeks away from a wedding with a few hundred guests. Ready or not, I was about to experience the most public outing of my life.

Nine

THE WEDDING
Exposed

Every mom dreams of her daughter's wedding day. When I was little my mama was a young working mom, and my daily "childcare" happened nowhere else than in the homes of Cedelia and Rose, my godly grandmothers. In their care my days were filled with cooking, exploring, reading, sewing, music, walks, Bible study, and gardening.

With my younger cousins I often visited the fantastic land of Long Closet in my grandma Rose's house; it was filled with early sixties bridesmaids' dresses and bridal gowns. My grandma had five daughters and three sons, which resulted in five brides between 1960 and 1966 and many, many bridesmaids' gowns, which demanded a closet all their own.

On hot days I would cool myself between the silky, pale pastel fabrics, letting them drape over me. At gatherings with my little girl cousins (or occasionally a willing boy cousin), I would don a bridal gown and dress them up as my powder blue, pale yellow, and peach-colored bridesmaids. Grandma Rose would quietly smile and bring us long white gloves, accessories, and hats from her bedroom to complete the ensembles.

These powerful memories accompanied me to the wedding of our daughter.

Her wedding was stunning. The venue was a gorgeous old ironworks building in Downtown Denver, with exposed brick and industrial details. Our daughter's vision and thoughtful details included the stunning floral design, with vintage hymnals and vintage photos of the bride and groom's parents' and grandparents' weddings. And Amanda, of course, was the most gorgeous bride I've ever laid my eyes on.

But one "detail" was missing that beautiful day. Her younger brother. He was in jail, and his absence left a giant-sized hole in our hearts. Although we had officially and respectfully appealed for a consideration to allow him to attend the ceremony, we were denied this privilege.

This day was a culmination of our entire year. Dread over one child's situation and anticipation for the other in a glorious, painful unfolding. A lifetime lived in a few short months.

We were determined to give ourselves fully to the joy of our daughter's wedding and not look all sackcloth and ash-y as we genuinely celebrated our precious, godly daughter's union to her sweet new husband and rejoiced in all that God had for them.

**Our hearts were simultaneously present
at the wedding celebration and in the county jail.**

The surreal celebration of joy came to a head in a private moment unbeknownst to all the wedding guests. During the reception Amanda's brother called, and we sweetly placed the phone to our daughter's ear so she could hear his voice above the banquet. I could barely breathe as I studied her face during their brief conversation.

I could hear Amanda tenderly assure him, "I love you . . . I love you too . . . I know . . . We'll dance together at your wedding . . . I love you." He loved her so much, and she loved him right back.

This was the public unveiling. Our friends and family were genuinely curious about his absence. Throughout the evening, over and over we were asked, "Where is Craig Jr.?" Since we were twenty-four days into his sentence, still getting our bearings, and had been planning a wedding, we had not yet "announced" our situation to the masses. No newsletter had gone out. No Facebook posts had declared, "Rough day. Our beloved son is in jail and we are in the final stretch of wedding prep for our daughter. Pray for us." I couldn't reduce our situation to small status updates.

Our big reveal happened in the most unexpected of places. It may sound like the absolute worst cloud over a joyous event, but it proved to be a huge relief.

Revealing our struggle was the biggest sigh of relief I'd ever known.

This wedding celebration began to lift the weight of our lonely world. It marked the beginning stages of the burden lifting off my shoulder, piece by piece, as we shared our reality with relatives and friends who loved us and loved our son deeply. Their sadness at the news helped lighten the burden of our own sadness. Their genuine love for our son broke our defenses. The pile of bricks on our shoulders was now shared with others, one small brick at a time.

Two are better than one, because they have a good reward for their toil. For if they fall, one will lift up his fellow. But woe to him who is alone when he falls and has not another to lift him up! Again if two lie together, they keep warm, but how can one keep warm alone? And though a man might prevail against one who is alone, two will withstand him —a threefold cord is not quickly broken.
—ECCLESIASTES 4:9–12 (ESV)

Tears once shed in lonely silence were now being wiped by the dearest of friends, who sat and extended boxes of Kleenex. This exposure came with unexpected beauty. We were no longer alone. We now experienced the unexpected sweetness and healing relief from sharing the journey with our dearest lifelong friends.

In addition to the deep work Scripture was working in my life, we needed the life-giving waters of the community of others. We needed to once again surround ourselves with the safety of people who loved Jesus, trusted in the Word, and deeply loved our family.

We needed to laugh again with the people who knew our laughable stories. We needed to lean against those we leaned on while raising our little tribe. We needed to love others and be loved in return.

As we moved forward from that moment, I knew He was still at work in my life. Strengthening my heart. Expanding my capacity. Connecting and reconnecting me.

**Dear reader, please hear me:
reconnection with community will multiply
the amount of prayer support,
which you desperately need.**

God designed us for meaningful, life-giving friendships.

Good, trusted friends are the ones with whom you don't have to work hard to fall back into step. The curtains drawn during my stiff-handed self-imposed isolation were thrown wide open, exposing the beauty of deep, lifelong friendships.

We had spent twenty-five years living under the waterfall of godly community. We knew firsthand the strength found in long-term, redemptive relationships. Together with the finest humans, we held fast to the importance of gathering, searching the Word together, prayer, and fun. We knew each other deeply.

We believed in the hard work of difficult relationship landscapes. We wholly believed in the longsuffering commitment that comes with long-lasting friendships.

Twenty-five years later, we still found the same things—except that we, all of us, had bled more and experienced more. Through the bleeding we had become even more aware of the goodness of God in our lives. We treasured the simple generosity of the God who had spread a banquet table before us. We now knew that all of life is a gift from our generous, loving Father, and our eyes were even more fixed on the goodness of God.

The big reveal was a reconnection with those who reminded me to take courage, who confronted the subtle lies I was attempting to uproot in my heart, and who reminded me of the beautiful "us" we had created together, back in the day, one goldfish cracker at a time.

From this point forward they were participants in bandaging my wounded and weary self. I had been knocked down a few notches, and they slowly helped prop me back up. They agreed with me regarding a bright future for my son. Expressing no doubt, they rehearsed the restoration ahead of him. They reminded me that God had a fully restored Plan A for him.

They noticed the goodness of God in my story. They encouraged me and praised God for his merciful work in our story. They actively breathed life into my story and made way for me to once again celebrate in all of our victories.

They lifted my face with their familiar hands. With their words they helped rebuild the rubble of my heart. With their memories they reminded me of the God-blessed moments of my life. They spoke plainly and truly, evidence of our older, wiser, and less authoritative stage of life.

I remembered the strength and design of authentic body life. Some of us are hands and some are feet. Some of us are really attentive ears, and some of us are filled with wise, careful words. Not one of us is the whole body by themselves. We belonged to one another, and I remembered that I could never fully be the God-glorifying mom I am without the support of other moms. I was meant to be my sisters' keeper, and they are mine.

I had weakened my own story when I reduced myself in isolation, when I refused to enter into the story with others and be a part of their hard won and precious successes. I fell into the huge trap of the enemy, which is to isolate and disconnect.

Community is filled with broken, imperfect people who allow God to enter our space and, for the glory of His name, work through us. Community allows us to make the most of the strength of others.

All your straining to see what is good and lovely will be quickly highlighted by your trusted friends. They see beauty where you see chaos. They will remind you of love and grace and courage and kindness wrapped in years and years of the hard stuff of life.

The sick feeling in the pit of my stomach was healed through the reverse silo-ing of my life.

For when I kept silent, my bones wasted away
through my groaning all day long.
For day and night your hand was heavy upon me;
my strength was dried up as by the heat of summer.
—PSALM 32:3–4 (ESV)

Parents, be brave. Take a chance and reconnect. The stress hormones in your body will thank you. Your health will thank you. Your very bones will thank you. Your weary, wrung-out body will thank you.

Your eyelashes will grow back.

Now, I'm not saying you should reconnect with every single person you've ever known. It's true that some people would make a discouraging situation even more discouraging, but if you have two or three trusted friends you have enough.

I'm talking about those who would clasp hands with you and hold back the storms of life if you let them. Those with whom you have deep, nuanced, face-to-face history. The relationships shaped by gracious love, day by day, struggle by struggle, memory by memory. For me, that meant three of my dearest women, part of our small group, who had survived with me the storms and beautiful pastures of nearly thirty years together.

Make time to laugh and eat and talk again. Your eyes will adjust to the brightness again. The exposing light of day will seem too bright at first, but you will get used to being fully seen. At first it will feel too bright, but you will reacquaint yourself with the brightness of safety and risk again.

As you reconnect with your community, don't underestimate the small gestures, texts, and baby steps. Remember, they have been waiting too.

Your community will remind you of the amazing things He has done in your life. Don't underestimate the power of good friends and good food wrapped in loyalty and years. Be safe again. Be trustworthy again by trusting.

It was a beautiful wedding. The flowers were yellow and white. Our precious daughter and son-in-law took the first steps in their beautiful journey as husband and wife. We missed our son in aching and terrible amounts. We renewed our journey of friendship with sweet friends from our Salad Days. *Selah.*

Ten

OUT OF THE ASHES
Do I See a Blossom on that Dead Tree?

Winters are long in Colorado. I'm not complaining, merely stating a fact. We get giddy when March rolls around, but I always want to wave my arms at new buds and blossoms that dare to peek out of tree branches and warn them to go back inside. I shake my head and warn, "Stop! Go back! A big storm is coming and will tear your new, tiny, inexperienced leaves to the ground!" We have been known to have fast and furious snowstorms near the end of May.

One early spring I gave in to the temptation to tuck my not-yet-de-winterized feet into sandals on an unseasonably warm day and slip into my favorite stores. After a brief visit to my favorite kitchen store, I lingered in the most glorious store of all time, and this fifty-year old mama of five's dreamy space: Anthropologie. This store speaks to me. It "gets" me. I even tuck in to their website now and then, and dream my own little virtual fantasies. Décor. Dresses. Floppy blouses. Fragrances. Hats. Shoes. Bags. Journals. Scarves. Linens. Ridiculously overpriced jeans. Books.

Delightful.

I was determined not to leave a stone unturned in my store, and

near the end of my excavation I found the travel book section. Destinations. Travel journals. Maps. Cities. Faraway places.

I hate travel journals. They mock me. Like a bikini competition
with large-bosomed women. My heart instantly felt the familiar pang
that whispers, "Your life is so small... You've never been anywhere..."

When I am in a particularly spicy mood, I feel like buying a travel
journal just to spitefully inscribe "Arvada, Colorado" in every single
page, using a thick ballpoint pen, allowing extra pressure for sarcastic
emphasis.

I picked up a journal and flipped through the empty pages, un-
sure of what had compelled me to pick them up. My hands ran over
the pockets reserved for tickets and memorabilia. I set it down and
picked up a book of maps. Another book. This one highlighted subway
systems.

And then I had a moment.

Out of the Anthropologie blue-green, I was reminded of *my* extensive and valuable travels: my life's journey of nurturing souls.
The adventure of attending to my own and others' search for God.
The discoveries of attending to my own faith and the faith of those
in my care.

My fellow travelers and tourists were my husband and my children. Stamps in our passports included the beauty of their everyday
lives and the home I have fashioned for them. The vulnerable looking
and listening for God along the way. The exploration of beauty and
sincerity. Of celebrating the goodness of God.

The journey of pain and loss. Of music expressed. Of loving deeply,
and being loved by others. The road trips of real relationships and the
experience of community. The snapshots of others. The other-ness of
my entire life, and its priceless rewards.

The small, deep destinations and the grand, sweeping mysteries
along the way.

There are beauty, glory, and unbridled enthusiasm in the mun-
dane.

It was then that I realized that the travel journals I held in my
hands were too small. The petite pages were not strong enough to hold
the vast worlds of my travels. And the adventures yet to come.

With satisfaction I set the book down and walked away.

**The journey I now found myself in turned out
to be the most satisfying of my life.**

For the next eleven months after the wedding, my new normal included lots and lots of car time with our son. The whirlwind of the first grueling eight months of the year settled into a surreal stillness at home, with our son in jail/work/college and our newlywed daughter approximately 2,041.9 miles away from us in a foreign land called Ft. Lauderdale.

My faith had been formed in the kitchens of my godly grandparents, and my children's faith was formed in my own kitchen. Kitchens had always been the sacred backdrop to my life's ministry. Feeding my family was (and still is) one of the best ways I knew to love and serve, and it became very important to me that I bring my son homemade, delicious, non-fast food every day. I needed to remind him, with his favorite meals, of the beauty of his secure place in our family and of his sonship. With each burrito I was laying a robe squarely on his shoulders.

Our frantic, fearful courtroom appearances were over. The hustle and bustle of wedding prep was behind us. What was left was a strangely peaceful "normal" life with our three younger children and our daily drives with our son. His work release schedule was in full swing, and it looked like this:

- ✓ Pick-up from county jail at 6 a.m. on inclement weather days, when he can't ride his bike, and drive son to work.
- ✓ Pick-up from work every day at 3 p.m., load his bike on bike rack, and drive him to college campus with homemade dinner from home, quickly enjoyed in the car on the way to campus.
- ✓ Pick up from college campus every evening at 8:30 p.m. by his grandmother (my mother, because she is full of so much love it's ridiculous),

with more homemade goodness, and return him
to county jail.
- ✓ Sleep.
- ✓ Repeat the next day and every single day for the
next eleven months.

Additionally, his Superman of a dad would pick him up every
Saturday with a plate of scrambled eggs and toast or a bowl of baked
oatmeal as together they drove to a county-mandated alcohol education class. His dad was also managing his commissary account
for food; helping with college resources when our son didn't have
access to resources; managing his college class schedule; making
tuition payments (along with wedding payments and legal fees);
and managing rent payments to the jail, as required by the work
release program. Basically, he served as the managing foreman for
this entire glorious operation.

**Jail was no match for the love
my family had for my son.**

Craig Jr. had a bike locked in front of the jail that he used to ride
to work, weather permitting, and I would pick him up after work
and mount the bike on the back of my Camry while we drove to his
campus. Every so often the bike would get a flat, and we would drive
to meet him and fix it like a Nascar pit crew. We were a well-oiled
machine.

He had what we now call "jail hands"—dry and cracked and dirty,
because he needed a hot shower and some lotion, for goodness sake.
Now, when I hold his hands and flip them over to reveal the underside,
I smile, remembering those rough jail hands.

It sounds brutal, but this season was sobering and redemptive
for my son, and therefore beautiful. He was a piece of solid gold,
enduring a refining fire. He suffered no ill effects from quitting
alcohol, marijuana, and antidepressants. God was so good and so
merciful. Our son was not bitter and defeated, but serious and de-

termined. He was grateful and aware of God's goodness. Something better was emerging.

The jail was a midwife.

The season was giving birth to deeper relationship and security. It was calm. I just remember it being crazy amounts of calm and predictability compared to the uncertain spinning-out-of-control season that preceded this one. Driving him in the car every day was an opportunity to silently speak hope, life, and Jesus into his life. I wanted him to know that God still had an outrageously amazing plan for his life, and the way to show him was to faithfully, daily, relentlessly love and serve him.

We drove in the beauty of quiet love and acceptance. The only urgency, besides the time restraints and check-ins, being the conveying and confirmation of love from parent to child. My fulltime job was now the taking care of our three young ones still at home, and of reminding my jailed son that he is still my beloved son in whom my favor rests. That was it. It was a simple, no-frills season of loving and serving and waking up the next morning and doing it again.

God's personal presence filled my humble car with His glory. It was holy ground. Sacred space. Uncrowded and quiet. We embraced the quiet by listening to one another. It was as though we were in a bubble of His presence, separated from the noise of the past, feeling the weight of God's steadfast love and faithfulness.

God encouraged, affirmed, and revealed a new reality of grace to us in the seats of that Toyota Camry. Mother and son, placed strategically at this intersection, paying close attention to the here-ness and now-ness of our situation. Each day new grace. Each day a new way of welcoming and affirming.

I had his full attention for the first time in a very long time, and we were both attentive to what God was doing in these new, compressed margins of time. Dignity was conferred in my car. Transactions of grace. Repair.

My son was matured, respectful, and responsible. Quiet and grateful and receptive. Instantly. From Day One. He was attentive and soft. With each trip the frozen layers were falling off our frosty relationship like scales. With each meal I placed in his lap, there was a melting. Healing.

I was acutely aware that the events I was witnessing were shaped by the presence and power of the Holy Spirit. The goodness and kindness of God were drawing our son closer to Himself, right before our eyes.

Not by might, nor by power, but by my Spirit, says the Lord of hosts.—ZECHARIAH 4:6 (ESV)

His beautiful eyes met mine as we talked about life, his job, his classes, the news of his sister in Florida, and his siblings at home. Sometimes I would bring Coco Chanel, and she would lick his face the entire time. Healing. Sometimes I would bring his younger siblings, and they would make him laugh. More healing. Sometimes he would drive the iPod music and would pick the *Hillsong Worship* album from his early high school years. More healing.

Each slight smile and eye contact was like a gentle kiss from heaven. They conveyed love. They spoke volumes upon volumes of hope.

I remained fully present in the here-ness and now-ness of the situation in which we found ourselves. I didn't dwell on the "What could we have done differentlies?" or concern myself with the "What lies aheads?" or, worst of all, engage in the conflict of "What is everyone else experiencing right now?" I allowed myself to fully savor each moment.

We once again visited memories from the Salad Days. We remembered how he had always had a small pocketknife tucked in his jeans and how he would search for any and every way to use it: cutting sticks and small, dead branches to build extravagant treasures. We remembered how he would spend endless days on the edges of his childhood pond, filling buckets with muddy turtles and snakes and tadpoles, presenting his discovered treasures to me with delight.

We remembered how one summer he had exclusively worn his "green shirt only," while the next he was married to his "shark shirt," and how I would launder them at night while he was sleeping.

The wilderness and the dry land shall be glad;
the desert shall rejoice and blossom like the crocus;
it shall blossom abundantly
and rejoice with joy and singing.
—ISAIAH 35:1–2 (ESV)

"Remember not the former things,
nor consider the things of old.
Behold, I am doing a new thing;
now it springs forth, do you not perceive it?
I will make a way in the wilderness
and rivers in the desert."
—ISAIAH 43:18–19 (ESV)

The season turned from late summer to autumn, and from autumn to winter. We slowly made our way around the bend and found the most beautiful and unexpected of all destinations: laughter.

I can still remember the spontaneous moment when we began to laugh again. Craig sometimes filled in as leader for a Bible study on Sunday nights in the jail, when the ministers who were scheduled to lead didn't show up. We laughed that all this drama was just an extravagant way for him to lead "jail ministry." It just made us laugh so hard. I couldn't remember the last time we had laughed together, and it was the sweetest, most healing laughing of my life.

Slowly the stranglehold on my throat loosened, and I could breathe again. I regained my voice. I found a new sense of possibility.

I felt the life returning to my worn-down body. I felt the spark of Jesus life returning to my son. He knew he was loved by his family. He knew there was no pit so deep that he would not remain our beloved son. He was grateful. There was no more hostility in our conversations. No more confusion and anger. He was walking back to us. In a car. In a jail cell. Walking back.

I knew Jesus wanted my prodigal son to live the deepest life possible—the fullest, richest life available. He wanted my prodigal to renew his relationship with the person and work of Jesus and to be reconciled to God the Father. He needed to daily know the magnitude of the mercy of God. The Lord wanted to lead my prodigal into a life of abundance and depth and meaning and purpose and peace. It was his decision alone, and I merely watched and rejoiced as it came to pass.

For me, the best way to love him was to wrap a plate of smothered green chili burritos, spaghetti pie, taco salad, or whatever else we were eating at home and hand it to him. This was our way of assuring him that he was ours and would always have a place at our table.

**It's almost absurd to think that this was
the sweet turning point in our story.**

Our child was in jail. We were at the mercy of this unbelievably harsh, merciful, sacred situation. His freedom was stripped. His wallet and phone were locked in a small locker outside every night. He slept in a room with twelve other men with the lights on. Our every pick-up and drop-off was monitored by a landline call to confirm his location. Random audits from the county sheriff confirmed his location.

Every few weeks I arrived at his job a few minutes early to speed shave his woolly mammoth hair situation in the sink of his work bathroom.

On Christmas Eve, knowing I wouldn't see him again until the day after Christmas, I parked in front of the jail around midnight, after our church's Christmas Eve service, and just sat in my car and cried, loving him and praying for him. I just cried. I called on the angels who appeared to the shepherds to come and appear to each and every man and woman locked in those jail cells and tell them to not be afraid—their story was not over. I prayed that the angels would tell each inmate that there is good news and great joy for them because a Savior came and was born for them.

I brought with me the words of the Christmas hymn we had ended our service with. The story of Jesus dripping over every single line of the song.

O HOLY NIGHT

written by Placide Cappeau de Roquemaure, 1847, © Public Domain

O Holy Night! The stars are brightly shining,
It is the night of the dear Saviour's birth.
Long lay the world in sin and error pining.
Till He appeared and the Soul felt its worth.
A thrill of hope the weary world rejoices,
For yonder breaks a new and glorious morn.
Fall on your knees! Oh, hear the angel voices!
O night divine, O night when Christ was born;
O night, O Holy Night, O night divine!

Led by the light of faith serenely beaming,
With glowing hearts by His cradle we stand.
O'er the world a star is sweetly gleaming,
Now come the wise men from Orient land.
The King of kings lay thus in lowly manger;
In all our trials born to be our friend.
He knows our need, to our weakness is no stranger,
Behold your King! Before him lowly bend!
Behold your King! Before him lowly bend!

Truly He taught us to love one another,
His law is love and His gospel is peace.
Chains he shall break, for the slave is our brother.
And in his Name all oppression shall cease.
Sweet hymns of joy in grateful chorus raise we,
Let all within us praise His holy name.

Christ is the Lord! Then ever, ever praise we,
His power and glory ever more proclaim!
His power and glory ever more proclaim!

He knows our need, so our weakness is no stranger. Weakness. Need. Heartache. Sickness. He knows. His very Presence was available that night. Breaking chains. Ending oppression. Imparting worth to our very souls.

As it turns out, my son was less traumatized over spending Christmas without us than I was. Laughing, he said, "I was way over-Christmased as a child." Funny, son. Real funny.

Winter gave way to spring, and soon we were counting down the weeks until his early summer release. A new and hopeful season was ahead.

Eleven months earlier, Craig and I had sat in these car seats and held the wallet, belt, and tie for a prodigal teenager, and now before us sat a man full of incredible courage, perseverance, and tenderness.

No travel journal could contain the beautiful sights of our daily adventures during those car rides. I saw tender blossoms peek out of dead branches, and I whispered to them, "Come on. You can do it."

Eleven

REBUILD
Welcome Home

As a small girl I loved Elvis. I loved him in a way I didn't even fully understand. To borrow from the Roberta Flack classic, with each note, he was "strumming my pain with his fingers, singing my life with his words, killing me softly with his song, telling my whole life with his words, killing me softly, with his song." Yes. I was that kind of a little girl, as far back as I can remember.

My early days with Elvis found me lifting myself up high on my tiptoes, reaching over my grandmother's stereo console cabinet, playing his gospel albums. Countless times.

As I lost myself in the songs, I would study the album cover, memorizing words along with every line of his beautiful, heaven-kissed face. He wore a white suit, a skinny white tie, and a blue shirt, perfectly matching the blue sky and white steepled panorama. He killed me softly with songs like "Peace in the Valley," "How Great Thou Art," and "He Touched Me." I was a small, smitten little girl.

In 1973 my mother announced that we were going to break tradition from my insanely early bedtime for a special event on TV. Up to this point in my life, the only time I had been allowed to stay up past my bedtime was to watch *The Ten Commandments* once a year. I remember sitting on the couch, with my older sister and Mom, waiting for the best scene, in our female minds, when Nefretiri falls at Charleston Heston's feet, pleading with him. We smiled in unison as we joined the Egyptian princess in chorus: "Moses, Moses, Moses!"

The reason for this unprecedented special late night was to watch Elvis's live from Hawaii TV special.

With head spinning and heart racing, I somehow managed to calm myself enough to take a nap, to ensure that I would not fall asleep during the concert. My Elvis. On TV. From Hawaii (wherever that is).

So there we were, three little Latinas, pink rollers securely set, scooted as close to our small TV console as possible. And then it happened. Elvis. The king himself. In all his glory. In my tiny living room. They showed a grainy graphic of a beeping white satellite somewhere deep in space, sending the signal straight to our home.

I couldn't believe my eyes, but my ears testified to the truth. It was him. Not as I knew him in his cherubic white gospel suit and skinny white tie. No, he wore a white jumpsuit with a big belt and sequined eagle wings. I was stunned and silent, but no less thrilled. I drank in every single song and kung-fu-style movement. For the first time my small ears heard songs like (hunk-a hunk-a) "Burnin' Love," "Suspicious Minds," and "Can't Help Falling in Love." I sat rapt during the entire concert, not daring to get up even for a quick restroom break, for fear of missing one note. It was pure heaven.

The day my son returned home I was singing songs of thanks and songs of home. You would think I would be humming Simon and Garfunkle's "Homeward Bound" or Michael Bublé's "Home." Nope. An obscure Elvis song filled my heart the day my son returned home.

GOING HOME
written by Joy Byers © unknown

I'm coming home, this time I'm gonna stay
I'm coming home and I ain't never goin' away
My feet are itching to get back home
I've had the desert fever since I've been gone

I need some loving so bad that I can't see
When a woman looks a man in the eye
You know it takes a man to satisfy
Thinking about them girls is killing me

I'm going home, going home
Going home, I'm going home
Going home, going home
Going home

He was released at midnight, and we picked him up at 12:01 and brought him home. His first drive without a landline check in eleven long months. We wanted to take him to Denny's for a proper middle-of-the-night celebration, but he just wanted to come home.

Home.

He needed to return to a place where he felt safe. He was exhausted from his long, pressing season and needed to feel a renewed sense of belonging here at home, beyond the passenger seat of our car. He needed to rest safely and quietly. With the lights off. He needed a warm shower. He was ready for a physical homecoming and a spiritual one.

He needed to feel the love from his younger brothers and sister.

There is a yearning in each of us that longs for the belonging found in home. There is a mystery of homecoming that strikes a deep chord within each of us. When we see a video of a soldier returning from war or deployment to surprise his waiting family with his homecoming, we are wrecked in a very real way. Total strangers, yet we are crying.

Home.

His homecoming was a rebuilding of his confidence in our family and a simultaneous pointing upward to his heavenly Father's love. It was a reclaiming of his unmerited sonship for himself. A laying his head on his own pillow. In his own bed. It was a spiritual rebuild and reframing upon the solid foundation of his life. We were now standing inside the walls of the best ever extreme home makeover as grateful overseers. Watching as the framing, wiring, plumbing, electrical, and drywall miraculously gave way to rooms.

His journey home had not been merely over the last eleven months. This was the culmination of every moment of his entire life. Every spiritual deposit was yielding a return. Every minute of investing in his heart. His unwasted spiritual reserve was rising to the surface.

Our home returned to a house of complete and profound love.

Our new normal included daily calls and check-ins for various parole requirements. He spent each day of his newfound freedom aware of its preciousness. He was serious and sober. Sweet. Smiling. Quiet and relieved. Creating new pathways and reacquainting himself with old, healthy ones.

We took a supporting role, watching from the sidelines, as in our football days, rejoicing with each victory. Thanking Jesus as he forged new paths of friendships and community. Leaning forward to watch him rise and succeed and have impact.

The natural path of supporting and cheering on a thriving young adult was now ours.

Eventually, he moved out with a roommate and plugged in to a church community. He once again enjoyed all things outdoors: hiking, biking, water skiing, snowboarding, adventuring, and fresh air.

About a year after his release, he met a sweet, godly girl named Abigail. She was the sixth daughter in a homeschooling family of all girls. The next year he received his bachelor's degree in accounting and continued in his work as manager and co-owner of a thriving business. He was once again fueled by a Spirit-filled power that was pushing him toward strength upon strength.

Building and rebuilding. Starting well. Finishing well. Thriving. Responsible.

Laughing.

Eventually, Abigail became his wife.

Together they now serve Jesus with their wild, blue-eyed husky dog, Tysen. They purchased an old, historic home near downtown Denver and are active in their local church. They share a love for adventure and the outdoors. They have huge, compassionate hearts for missions and for raising their own family.

Last September they welcomed the birth of their newborn son. She had a prophetic dream that this child would be a Revival Child. His name is Craig, just like his dad and his grandpa. A legacy of godly men. Amen.

God went extravagantly above and beyond *all* I could think or imagine in his restoration. He was over the top in his bringing our son fully home. We knew God absolutely had a plan for our child. It was a brutally rough and rocky road, but his was a victorious story of reconciliation.

When your prodigal child returns to serving Jesus, it is often the realest serving you've ever seen. They don't do fake anymore because they lived that fake life during their descent and have no use for it. They live full and truthful lives.

During his journey we learned the greatest and hardest lessons in patience and perseverance. We asked God to do a profound work in our son, and he ended up doing a profound work in all of us. We wanted our son to know and savor Jesus and to once again know that he is fully forgiven and deeply loved by his heavenly Father and his earthly parents.

He was home.

We were all home.

Twelve

HOME

I set up Christmas trees in October filled with all manner of pump-kins and harvest bounty and autumnal-leafed garland. I replace the harvest bounty with Christmas ornaments in mid-November and leave it up as long as humanly possible after December 25. If you know someone who is similarly wired, let me give you some inside information: they cannot be shamed. You can Christmas-shame them all you want, and it rolls off their backs like water on a pear-tree-perched partridge.

I lovingly refer to myself as a Christmas enthusiast, and as far as I can tell I descended from a long line of Christmas enthusiasts. My mama raised me in the full glory of an entire section of her closet reserved for glorious Christmas sweaters, Joslin's boxes filled with festive Christmas jewelry to perfectly accessorize said Christmas sweaters, Nat King Cole albums, Department 56 Dickens Christmas Villages, Christmas décor, outdoor lights, multiple ridiculously gor-geous trees, and a long list of delicious Christmas cookie standards.

My mother's biscochitos are the single most delicious Christ-mas cookie ever known. Who knew that you could throw together flour, baking powder, salt, lard, sugar, eggs, toasted and crushed anise seeds, and orange juice, and roll it out to form the most heavenly anise-and-cinnamon-sugar-scented cookies on earth?

My unofficial daily to-do list in December looks like this:

- ✓ Make coffee
- ✓ Read Advent journal while enjoying 2 biscochitos
- ✓ Shop for presents online
- ✓ 2 more biscochitos as a reward
- ✓ Wrap presents
- ✓ 2 biscochitos to replenish energy from wrapping

You get the general idea.

When November rolls around, after my strings of lights are tested and my garland is fluffed and readied, I lay my ornaments gently on the couch and reminisce as I unwrap each sacred and delightful piece.

I'll never forget the days gone by when my kids would gather around the nativity sets and I would remind them of each beloved character. In the final moment we would unwrap baby Jesus and remind ourselves of how God loved us SO much that He sent his son, Jesus, and that Jesus loved us SO much that he died for our sins.

See why I love Christmas so much?

To this day I have no baby Jesuses in my nativity sets because my kids would take him and hide him, or sleep with him under their pillows—I honestly don't know what they would do with him, but the tiny figure eventually disappeared.

There are some young parents who will bend low on both knees and tell their precious babes "Jesus loves you" and all will go well. There are others of us who will be asked to walk through dark valleys, without knowing the end of the story, and we will be more beautifully and painfully anchored to the words "Jesus loves you" than we ever imagined.

Parents of prodigals, you are not alone. So many of us have waited in the same place. Silently. Expectantly. Fearfully.

No two prodigal journeys look the same. For some of you the

epic rock bottom is a long way off, and you may be in the early stages of "I have a bad feeling about this." For some of you it seems that rock bottom is where you have remained for years and perhaps decades.

You will make mistakes one moment, and the next you will get it incredibly right by the grace of God.

The same way each family is unique, each family waiting for a prodigal is unique. Varying levels of heartache touch each story.

Don't stop waiting. Don't stop serving them. Pray the psalms. Remember Luke 15.

Some of you have endured the pain of addiction, rejection, estrangement, unplanned teenage pregnancies, and all manner of situations not even touched in this book. You may have other children to love and care for, or you may be alone as you wait. Your prodigal child may be like the handling of an explosive device, or he may be living a very loud silence.

Don't give up.

Regardless of where you are, and how you're suffering, dear parents of prodigals, know that He is closer than you think and more powerful than you can imagine.

The path of parenting comes with excruciating amounts of uncertainty and risk, but know, dear reader, that you are not alone on this path. God is faithful.

Hope deferred makes a heart really, really sick. Whether it's a wandering child or a lost dream, there is a sickness. I'm here to tell you that the same mercy and grace of Jesus, who brought my family through the darkest valley, is available for you. He is available in each and every broken situation. He is with you the whole time, waiting for you to become aware of His Presence.

I wish I could have painted a more flattering portrait of myself in the waiting. The reality of our own fallen nature is a player in this story. The truth is that He was preparing a table before me, and I came to the table kicking and screaming. He faithfully waited as I waded through the rivers of self to emerge humbled and ready to serve. He entrusted me with this beautiful journey, and I will never be the same.

During this prodigal season we spent plenty of time bumping into the walls and bumping into each other. It was very disorienting. But through it all we discovered and rediscovered God's heart for our child and began participating and cooperating with what the Spirit of God was doing in our prodigal's life. We stooped down low and walked beside him and served him.

His capacity to work through you is not limited by your own brokenness.

Like the shepherd and the woman with the lost coin and the prodigal's father in Luke 15, we got muddy, dusty, and undignified in our pursuit.

> *Obey God and leave the consequences to Him.*
> —CHARLES STANLEY

Parents of prodigals, be courageous and strong. Let's continue to talk deeply and truthfully about Jesus and his love for our children. Let's steward our stories well.

I'm officially middle-aged now. As far as I can tell, that means the age at which I'm starting to buy jars of face cream with print so fine my middle-aged eyes can't read the details. The age at which my bottle of L'Oreal Dark Brown Number 4 is the most consistent bimonthly friend I have. The age where my right eyelid is sending me a November warning flag of distress.

At nearly fifty-two, I find myself in the early autumn of life. I love autumn. The hot evenings slowly give way to crisp and cool nights, and the heat-scorched Colorado landscape turns yellow and orange and red. I pull on hats and scarves and tuck my jeans inside my boots like a hug at the end of a long day. I look for any and every excuse to buy canned pumpkin, and I love, love, love the sound of the wind through the golden aspen trees as they applaud the goodness of God. It bids me to notice.

The autumn season of my life has been the same. I'm paying attention like never before.

The things that served me well in my early years are now behind me. Because of my journey as a prodigal's mom, I can no longer live the same way I did in the early days. Beyond being sage and mellow, I have a Spirit-breathed resilience and grit I never knew before. I understand just what matters in life.

I know who I am and what He has called me to and what drives me. I feel renewed confidence in following Jesus, the source of my life. I feel the shaping and celebrating of His call on my life and my mothering. I want to love my family more, because Jesus is the absolute source of my life. I consider my time, my influence, and my moments even more deeply.

I will never be the same. I measure my life in two segments: before this prodigal journey and after. I lost my life in the journey. I came out on the other side humbled, more compassionate, quieter, and more attentive. My trust in God is giant-sized for our future. I've seen Him come through in the past, and I believe he will do it over and over and over.

Our son might have walked the straight and narrow of a very neat and tidy trajectory, and I might have missed out on the ever-increasing joy and deep work of a lost son found by the grace of God. There are measures of His presence you can find only while walking through valleys. There is unusual grace to be found in desert places.

The journey described in these pages brought me to a new understanding of my calling as a parent and offered me new strength to live it. Through this journey I came to know the boundlessness of God's compassionate love. The journey refined what I believed about who God is, His nature, and His character.

God is who he says He is.
He is good. His promises endure.

My ideas of my tomorrows were redirected to His loving wisdom alone. My fragile self was held together by His generous abundance. The goodness of God was confirmed and reconfirmed in my life because of the cross. His heart is to rescue and ransom us over and over.

I understood and acknowledged my weakness because I had no choice. He exposed my arrogance and pride for His truly good purposes. He lovingly revealed my shortcomings over and over again. I learned to walk in patience, simply because I couldn't stay in bed.

I became a more humble and graceful person, less inclined to look down upon anyone else. I'm approachable and patient because of the truths worked out over and over in my life and solidified through this prodigal journey. The *experience* of the truth is very different from merely knowing the truth.

I learned that for a life lived pursuing Christ I still needed to pursue wisdom and humility, and that at the end of the day's pursuit there will still be more to learn. I learned to walk in patience, and at the end of the day I learned I had a million miles still to go. I moved forward in obedience and joy, knowing there were greater and greater things ahead than I had ever known possible.

I learned that the invitation to come to Jesus, commune with Him, and learn of Him is fresh every morning. All areas of my life needed a fresh communion.

God is faithful. He can do amazing things.

I learned that daily immersion in the Word and in prayer is not just a duty but a delight and a gift. Read, speak, and pray the Word of God over your circumstance and affirm its truth over and over and over.

I learned that whether I'm suffering or rejoicing over a son who is walking over the horizon back home, He is there.

My prayer life is deeper now and less systematic. My confession life is truer and less padded.

There are a lot of parenting books that say a lot of things, but good old-fashioned longsuffering goes a long way.

This journey shaped my family. This crucible made us more aware of our need for God. It made us grateful for the life of our son. For every dark night there is morning. For every devastating pile of ashes there is beauty. I trust that our Christ-exalting story will encourage parents who are waiting, the ones who are setting a holiday table with one painfully empty seat.

I pray that the fruit of our suffering, sown with isolated tears, will yield a beautiful garden as Jesus replaces with beauty the ashes of what we have endured.

Beloved, He is closer than you think and more powerful than you can imagine. I encourage you to daily depend on His grace and mercy as you wait. And do it again when you wake up tomorrow. Remember that Jesus has not grown weary of His love for your prodigal. He is all about the restoration of humanity and the restoration of our wandering children. You are not alone.

I recognize that you are fighting on many fronts: the battle for yourself, the battle for your prodigal child, the battle for your other children, and the battle for your home. When your child is on a journey, *you* are on a journey.

Remember that as He is bringing your child home He is working in you and in the life of your child. He is maturing you and growing you through the homecoming season. He is conforming you to the image of his Son, Jesus. He is actively at work in your heart.

I'm asking God to bring freedom, wholeness, and healing to all those in the waiting.

You're exhausted and limping. You may feel marginalized and unsuitable. Everything you feel is shaped by loss. While you are waiting it's difficult to find solid footing. But remember that while you are in the dark space between the already and the not-yet *He is with you.*

I once prayed an audacious prayer for my son. I was tempted to pray the small, reasonable prayers of "please help him get back on the rails" and "please help him live a law-abiding life" and "please break unhealthy relationships when he is released from jail." Instead I prayed for miraculous transformation. I prayed that he would be an over-the-top, unrecognizable extension of the severely courageous, godly young man I once knew. I prayed that he would renew his passion for changing the world. That he would step into his unique, God-given purpose and potential and be a giant killer. That he would run wholeheartedly into the who God created him to be. I prayed that something would emerge both recognizable and renewed. I prayed outside the boundaries of conventional, small expectations. My prayers were more than a wishful plea that restoration would be possible; I prayed for something even better than existed before.

I prayed that he would realize his full spiritual potential, not his Plan B potential.

It came to pass. Slowly. Excruciating amounts of slow. But it came to pass. God is slow, careful, and compassionate. He isn't in the business of quick fixes in the lives of your children.

My prodigal child is home. His life is a living, breathing, authentic expression of hope. His life is evidence that you can overcome spiritual brokenness and not remain broken. He daily reminds me that God is faithful to accomplish every good work he began in us and through us.

Parenting a wayward child doesn't have to be the end of your story. God still wants to use your life to lift and lead others to Himself.

God will make possible what was impossible with man. Give God room to show Himself faithful. When I see my son's life and observe him living abundantly in his God-given purpose, I want to pinch myself. God has done a remarkable, stunning work.

Hold tight. Be patient. Every moment of anxiety, worry, suffering, and humiliation will be worth it. God is accomplishing something great in you. Look to the cross. Then look again.

Jesus never wearies of our struggling. The steadfast love of the Lord endures. He is paying attention. He is leaning into your brokenness with His compassion. His promises are true. He is stepping into your space, saying, "Hang in there. Don't let go. I never will."

"Now to him who is able to do far more abundantly than all that we ask or think, according to the power at work within us, to him be glory in the church and in Christ Jesus throughout all generations, forever and ever. Amen."—EPHESIANS 3:20–21 (ESV)

SECTION TWO

Twenty-One Day Devotional

Twenty-One Day Devotional

My grandparents died when I was seven years old. They were the greatest spiritual influence of my life, and I only enjoyed their flesh-and-blood earthly relationship during my first few (formative) years. I remember sitting with them in the sacred space of our small breakfast table with Bibles opened, over-medium eggs and New Mexico red chili, a folded tortilla on the side, and ribbons of steam ascending from their coffee mugs.

I watched their leathered hands smooth precious worn pages with reverence as they read aloud in Spanish from their Santa Biblias and then as they prayed INTO them and OVER us. My small brown hands would fold in front of me, imitating the sounds I heard, absorbing the thick, Spirit-breathed atmosphere and their thick, accented words.

Like the ribbons of coffee steam, the incense of their prayers ascended every morning. The heavenly petitions breathed at that humble breakfast table continue to mark my life. Momentum was created for generations. Their prayers continue to mark me, move me, and shape me. I have now lived long enough to see the activity of their prayer continue in the lives of my children and grandchildren. The prayers of my grandparents outstripped their lives and shaped my destiny.

If you peel back the curtains of space and time and unveil the battle plan for my life, these morning breakfast scenes would most certainly be command central.

"Truly I tell you, whatever you bind on earth will be bound in heaven, and whatever you loose on earth will be loosed in heaven.

"Again, truly I tell you that if two of you on earth agree about anything they ask for, it will be done for them by my Father in heaven."—MATTHEW 18:18–20 (NIV)

My grandfather was a pastor and a kingdom giant in the pulpits, but his lasting impact in my life took place in the humble seats at a simple kitchen table. The pulpit marked my heritage, but the kitchen table marked my destiny. Here's the simple lesson I learned at that long-ago breakfast table: pray. Pray in the *will* of God, for the *glory* of God, informed by the *Word* of God.

My grandparents prayed prophetically into and over my life. They prayed without ceasing. They wrote my future with their prayers.

But the mercy of the LORD is from everlasting to everlasting
On those who fear Him,
And His righteousness to children's children.—PSALM 103:17 (NKJV)

My spiritual inheritance causes me to know without a doubt that my prayers are effective.

I will pray the promises of God over my children all my days. These prayers will be the inheritance I leave them.

My prodigal child was a prayed for child.

I interceded for his future spouse. I believed for miracles. I prayed with an ache for what God alone could do in his life. I pursued and prayed for the heart and will of God to be accomplished in him and through him. I prayed hedges and hedges of protection around him. I prayed outrageous abundance for him. Springs in the desert. Blossoms on dead trees.

I added this small prayer devotional as a summary of the main themes I prayed during our battle days. These meditations could not serve as a separate chapter because they wove themselves through the fabric of the entire story. I offer no "how-to" other than to get up. Get dressed. Open your Bible. Pray without ceasing.

I fought the greatest battle of my life with prayer. It was the only weapon I had—and it was more than enough!

Rise during the night and cry out.
   Pour out your hearts like water to the LORD.
Lift up your hands to him in prayer,
   pleading for your children.—LAMENTATIONS 2:19 (NLT)

It comes the very moment you wake up each morning. All your wishes and hopes for the day rush at you like wild animals. And the first job each morning consists simply in shoving them all back; in listening to that other voice, taking that other point of view, letting that other larger, stronger, quieter life come flowing in. And so on, all day . . .— C. S. LEWIS

Day One

TEACH US TO PRAY

One day Jesus was praying in a certain place. When he finished, one of his disciples said to him, "Lord, teach us to pray, just as John taught his disciples."

He said to them, "When you pray, say:
'Father,
hallowed be your name,
your kingdom come.
Give us each day our daily bread.
Forgive our sins,
   for we also forgive everyone who sins against us.
And lead us not into temptation.'"—LUKE 11:1–4 (NIV)

This prayer devotional highlights my personal scratching of the surface of prayer through our prodigal season. My grandparents were kingdom giants and four-star prayer generals, and by no means have I reached their expert level. Mine was a messy, gut-wrenching spiritual guerilla warfare training, for sure, and I am slowly, gracefully earning my stripes.

In my Bible I have a prayer card that walks through the Lord's Prayer, line by line. It's a good place to start for so many reasons, mainly because Jesus himself said, "When you pray, say . . ."

Take a moment and thank Him for being your Father. Remember that God is a good Father who loves each of His children uniquely. Starting here, in this position, frees us from distrust. Thank Him for the benefits of His Name. He is our healing, provision, and peace. He is present, our banner and our shepherd. He is our righteousness and sanctification.

Realize that our standing is not based on what we've done or not done, on the level of our effort or our accomplishments. Our standing is secure in the work of Jesus alone.

Ask Him to extend His Lordship over every part of your life, and agree with His will.

Thank Him for His provision over every area of our daily need.

Confess your sins and trust His faithfulness to forgive. Release resentments, grudges, and bitterness against others.

Trust that He has made a way of escape for us so we will not enter into temptation when it comes our way.

Prayer

Father, thank you for my position as your child and for the gift of your Son to make my sonship a reality. I focus my vision on the greatness of your Name and all the benefits of that great Name. I pray that your kingdom will come and your great will be done in every area of my life. I trust you as my provider for this day. Forgive the sins I've committed against you alone. You are faithful to forgive me. Your Word links my relationship to you and to others, so I gladly release sins and offenses against others. Thank you for making a way of escape and for the deliverance that comes from you alone. Amen.

Day Two

INCREASE OUR FAITH

Then he said to him, "Rise and go; your faith has made you well."
—Luke 17:19 (NIV)

[Jesus] said to her, "Daughter, your faith has healed you. Go in peace and be freed from your suffering." —Mark 5:34 (NIV)

So then faith comes by hearing, and hearing by the word of God.
—Romans 10:17 (NKJV)

I began this small prayer devotional by describing my grandparents' rich kitchen table prayer-scape, complete with open Bibles. Their simple dependence *on* Him and their utter expectation to receive all they needed *from* Him was informed by the Scripture they rehearsed and clung to. This was the simple exercise and development of their beautiful faith.

During our prodigal season, I hoisted the prayer sail forged by my grandparents' faith and moved with the wind of God as daily it carried me.

Faith is an overwhelming confidence that God IS who He says He is. It is a response to His very nature and His Word.

Their faith was strong not because they closed their eyes tight and "wished" upon a thing with all their might but rather because they were intimate with Scripture. As they meditated on the words of Scripture, they trusted the illuminating work of the Spirit to reveal its truth, and from there they simply prayed.

They quietly exuded confidence in the Father, and their rich, faith-filled prayer life was the result of surrender, not striving. Their souls were anchored and at rest in the midst of chaos. Their relationship with the Spirit led to greater confidence in the Father. Their faith pleased the Father.

Their faith was strong, and therefore their prayer life was strong.

Prayer

Father, increase our faith and teach us to pray. We trust you for great things by faith, knowing that it all rests on your great power and ability. As we trust you, we ask you to increase our faith. Increase our confidence in you. Thank you for the truth found in your Word. Amen.

Day Three

ASK

"And whatever you ask in My name, that I will do, that the Father may be glorified in the Son. If you ask anything in My name, I will do it."—JOHN 14:13–14 (NKJV)

Now this is the confidence that we have in Him, that if we ask anything according to His will, He hears us. And if we know that He hears us, whatever we ask, we know that we have the petitions that we have asked of Him.—1 JOHN 5:14–15 (NKJV)

I'm not going to deny the fact that these verses make many people squeamish. I'm also not going to deny that God often performs the miraculous in cooperation with our prayer.

Jesus initiated the invitation. He longs to perform great works by pouring a spirit of supplication on us so that we participate with His work.

When we pray, we are to pray according to His will (with an open Bible) and with the confidence that He hears us. When God hears our prayer, He is not affirming the person who prayed or even the thing prayed for; He is affirming His own Word and blessing us with peaceful lives while He's at it. He is glorifying the Father.

Confidently pursue the heart and will of God.

Pray with an ache for what He alone can do. Don't pray AT situations with accusation, but pray FOR people in cooperation with what the Spirit can do.

Prayer

Father, we ask according to your will. We know, according to 1 Timothy 2:4, that you desire for all to be saved and come to the knowledge of the truth. We ask with bold confidence, knowing that you hear our prayer. We ask that you would be glorified. We ask in your name, Jesus. Amen.

Day Four

WAITING

It is good to wait quietly
for the salvation of the LORD.—LAMENTATIONS 3:26 (NIV)

But those who wait on the LORD
Shall renew their strength;
They shall mount up with wings like eagles,
They shall run and not be weary,
They shall walk and not faint.—ISAIAH 40:31 (NKJV)

None who wait for you shall be put to shame.—PSALM 25:3 (ESV)

Have you noticed that traffic patterns are delayed in the age of smart phones? When waiting at a red light, the time it takes for the effect of a green light to slowly reach you if there are a few cars in front of you is basically for.ever. because every.single.person took out their phone and got lost in the black hole of "productive" email/text/social media as they were waiting for the light. There is no such thing as quietly waiting at an intersection with your hands on the wheel. Those days are basically gone.

Waiting is hard. We long to make use of the time while we wait.

Waiting for something significant feels like the worst waste of time.

Trust is cultivated in seasons of waiting. Waiting in an atmosphere of faith leads to greater trust, while waiting in an atmosphere of doubt leads to despair. God says that "it is good to wait" because He is producing something beautiful as we wait.

Strength is cultivated in seasons of waiting. If you find yourself in the grip of profound weariness, there is renewed strength to be found by simply waiting on the Lord. God wants to perfect His strength in the utter weakness revealed during seasons of waiting.

God is all about making use of the time. He is accomplishing great things in the life of your child, your family, and your own heart as you wait. He never wastes seasons of waiting.

Waiting seasons rarely "feel" good, but rest in the assurance that God is accomplishing great things.

Prayer

Father, as I wait, give me the grace to trust your faithful working. Though it's hard to be patient, I believe that you are moving on behalf of our child and our family. Give me patience and grace to keep trusting you in the face of impossible situations. I cling to you in this waiting season. Amen.

Day Five

GRACE TO THE HUMBLE

But he gives us more grace. That is why Scripture says:

> *"God opposes the proud*
> *but shows favor to the humble."*—JAMES 4:6 (NIV)

Humility is not the same as humiliation. It's possible to trip and fall and have your face covered in dirt and still walk away angry and prideful.

Humility is about becoming more and more like Jesus.

A proud spirit resists God and the work of God in our lives. God opposes the proud because he longs to be close to us and show favor to us. He longs to pour out grace upon us. Humility allows His Spirit to correct, teach, and cure our hearts.

Prideful hearts resist the work of the Spirit.

Jesus came to humbly serve, even though he is the King of creation. He was marked by fierce, brave-hearted resolve even while walking in great humility. His gentleness and grace are poured out when we spend more time with Him. He shows us favor as we serve others in humility.

God is waiting to give you more grace and favor. He is waiting to pour out good things in your life.

Prayer

Father, forgive me for my prideful heart. Give me the grace to serve others. Help me long for you more than I long for comfort and ease. Release me from the trap of comparison as I humbly serve those you've called me to love. Amen.

Day Six

BATTLE

*For we wrestle not against flesh and blood, but against princi-
palities, against powers, against the rulers of the darkness of
this world, against spiritual wickedness in high places.*
—EPHESIANS 6:12 (KJV)

*Then Jesus came to them and said, "All authority in heaven and
on earth has been given to me."*—MATTHEW 28:18 (NIV)

If you've made it this far in this devotional for parents of prodigal
children, you are passionate about seeing your child delivered and
healed. Your boots are most certainly on the ground in the Spirit
as you seek clarity and freedom. You understand that the weapons
of our warfare are mighty to pull down strongholds. You are committed to fight this battle with the sword of the Spirit, which is the
Word of God.

While you battle, don't give the wrong things permission and
strength. Don't be a reflection of what you "see" in flesh and blood,
but live with hope and confidence, regardless of circumstances.

Remember that God is the strong One in the battle. According
to Matthew 28, ALL authority has been given to Jesus. The enemy
has power, but the only authority he has is the authority we give

him when we agree with him. We sign things over to him by agreeing with him.

Don't give the enemy permission. Break agreements you've made that undermine the very battle you are fighting. Trust in the authority that has been given to Jesus.

Remember that God is the strong One in the battle.

Don't crawl on the floor in battle-worn defeat. Stand up, shoulders back, chin up, and trust the authority given to Jesus.

Prayer

Father, thank you for the work of the cross of Jesus and for the ultimate battle won. Remind us daily that we can't have authority over things with which we are in agreement. You are the victorious One, and I thank you for giving me a firm place to stand in the midst of this battle and for being our champion. Amen.

Day Seven

CONNECT

Two are better than one, because they have a good reward for their toil. For if they fall, one will lift up his fellow. But woe to him who is alone when he falls and has not another to lift him up! Again if two lie together, they keep warm, but how can one keep warm alone? And though a man might prevail against one who is alone, two will withstand him — a threefold cord is not quickly broken. —ECCLESIASTES 4:9–12 (ESV)

Colorado winters can be harsh. The crazy thing is, spring can be harsh as well, so basically half the year rests somewhere between cold and bitter cold. A typical winter or spring day can be mind-numbing, windshield-ice-scraping cold in the morning and sunny by afternoon.

This leaves you (mostly) uncertain of how to appropriately dress.

Have you ever found yourself underdressed in the cold? You underestimated the weather and found yourself sitting on the freezing bleachers of a sports event with no gloves, hat, or appropriate socks? Then some crazy generous (and well-prepared) person hands you their spare blanket or extra coat, and you sheepishly accept the kind gesture.

Isolation is a huge tactic of the enemy in the life of a believer. Isolating yourself during the painful season of waiting for your prodigal child feels like self-preservation. It actually exposes us to the cold, however, and we were created for community—especially when we are cold. While you are waiting between the now and the not-yet, remember that you were created for meaningful, life-giving friendships. You were designed for redemptive relationships with others who will point your hurting heart back to Jesus.

Prodigal seasons pull us inward. They leave us feeling marginalized and unsuitable. Jesus is leading you back to friendship with a few faithful people who will remind you that you are seen, safe, secure, and loved. He is inviting you to reconnect with a trusted friend who will remind you that God is faithful to accomplish every good work He began in us and through us.

Open your heart. Take the risk of friendship's path once again. Open yourself to a trusted friend who reminds you that God is good, that there is no other place as safe as remaining firmly in His will, and that He works everything out for our good. His will is always immeasurably, unspeakably, infinitely beyond our greatest expectation.

Invite someone to come and sit with you again. Invite them to come beside you and keep watch with you.

Accept the gesture of a warm blanket, and don't miss out on the opportunity to give someone your gloves or hat as they are sitting in the cold.

Father, your design is that we would most certainly be our brother's keeper. You knew we would need the warmth of faithful friendships. Thank you for creating us for community and for the friends you've entrusted to us along the way. Thank you for redeeming our relationships and making a way for us to love and serve others and to receive love from them in return. Amen.

Day Eight

WAY MAKER

"Forget the former things;
    do not dwell on the past.
See, I am doing a new thing!
    Now it springs up; do you not perceive it?
    I am making a way in the wilderness
and streams in the wasteland."—ISAIAH 43:18–19 (NIV)

It's interesting that one of the meanings of the word *dwell* means "to think or speak of something in great length," like brooding. Another meaning of the word refers to "a place you inhabit or live in." Oftentimes, one leads to the other. When you dwell on something, it becomes the place you dwell.

I can fall into a nostalgic hole like no other person could ever begin to understand. When I'm at a particularly low point, I will drive myself to a local antique mall and sloooowly shuffle through the aisles, examining worn albums, memorabilia, and trinkets that most people would have tossed in the trash decades ago. It's not my best self.

We dwell on the past because it seems better than our current state. Ironically, at the same time, we dwell on the past because it was horrible, and it keeps us stuck. Either way, God is calling us, inviting us, and giving us permission to forget the former things and fix our eyes on a new thing.

Oftentimes, when our situation is bleak, we long for the secure feelings associated with the past.

God wants to invite you to leave the security of the past and make way for a new thing. He is inviting you to witness new things that have never been seen before. He is making a fruitful way in situations that are barren and desolate, where there is absolutely no way (from our limited perspective).

He is our way maker and our stream giver.

Prayer

Father, I set my eyes forward and thank you for your work of love in redeeming humankind. You are the way maker. I thank you for the good future you have prepared for us. Thank you for making a way in the dry wilderness and for providing streams in the parched wasteland. Amen.

Day Nine

FORGIVE

Be kind to one another, tenderhearted, forgiving one another,
even as God in Christ forgave you. —EPHESIANS 4:32 (ESV)

If you've lived on the planet Earth for more than five minutes, you've likely experienced an offense from which you must extend forgiveness. If you've lived more than twenty years on the planet, you've collected more offenses than can be counted.

Prodigal families experience a unique measure of offenses.

Forgive.

Live unoffended lives and remember that Jesus' death on the cross satisfied the Father's justice.

Take time to fully extend forgiveness. Set the tone in confusing atmospheres and serve others by extending forgiveness. Walk each and every day remembering that kindness and consideration of one another matter. Extend peace and goodwill and grace-giving forgiveness even when bent over from cruel gut-punches. Wake up the next day resolved to extend it again, based on the work of Jesus alone.

Resolve to remain open hearted and tender to His voice.

Knowing that this fractured, broken world isn't going to be fully fixed until His kingdom comes and all things are renewed, welcome the beauty of this side, knowing that He is ever at work *in* us and *through* us. Each day He invites us to participate anew in the Spirit's work on earth and in our hearts.

Practice forgiveness so that it becomes second nature. Let it be your default position. If you don't get it right today, know that you'll likely be handed another opportunity to forgive before the week's end.

Prayer

Father, you know every broken situation in this journey. I fully rest in your forgiveness, and I extend forgiveness for every cruel offense. I seek to make room for my prodigal child to rise and succeed and have impact, and I choose to make room by forgiving all offenses and by seeking forgiveness. Thank you for the opportunity to know you in this way of forgiveness. Amen.

Day Ten

BE PATIENT

*Be patient, therefore, brothers, until the coming of the Lord. See how the farmer waits for the precious fruit of the earth, being patient about it, until it receives the early and the late rains. You also, be patient. Establish your hearts, for the coming of the Lord is at hand. Do not grumble against one another, brothers, so that you may not be judged; behold, the Judge is standing at the door. As an example of suffering and patience, brothers, take the prophets who spoke in the name of the Lord. Behold, we consider those blessed who remained steadfast. You have heard of the steadfastness of Job, and you have seen the purpose of the Lord, how the Lord is compassionate and merciful.—*JAMES 5:7–11 (ESV)

Patience is so much more than "staying calm." Some of the words associated with patience are *longsuffering, slowness, steadfastness,* and *forbearance.* None of these words seems to be related to calmness, but rather to staying the course.

The farmer must be patient in order to see precious fruit, but he doesn't simply need to remain calm. Patience isn't merely a state of passive detachment but an expectant waiting for precious fruit. It is an understanding and trusting in the transformative work of early and late rains.

Patience works through steadfastness and reveals the compassion and mercy of the Lord.

During the waiting season, patience is a game changer. It's not a stooped over position of resignation but a steady, expectant posture of trust. Trust that God is not slow. Trust that He is ever faithful and at work.

Patience is leaning in and paying attention.

Henri Nouwen describes patience like this:

Patience is a hard discipline. It is not just waiting until something happens over which we have no control: the arrival of the bus, the end of the rain, the return of a friend, the resolution of a conflict. Patience is not a waiting passivity until someone else does something. Patience asks us to live the moment to the fullest, to be completely present to the moment, to taste the here and now, to be where we are. When we are impatient we try to get away from where we are. We behave as if the real thing will happen tomorrow, later and somewhere else. Let's be patient and trust that the treasure we look for is hidden in the ground on which we stand.

Let us be patient.

Prayer

Father, I pray for the longsuffering kind of patience that yields precious fruit. I thank you for the grace to endure and the work of patience. Give me the peace that comes from knowing you are creating something precious. I rest in knowing that every good thing comes from you. Amen.

Day Eleven

JOY IN HEAVEN

"Just so, I tell you, there will be more joy in heaven over one sin-
ner who repents than over ninety-nine righteous persons who
need no repentance."—LUKE 15:7 (ESV)

"In the same way, there is joy in the presence of God's angels
when even one sinner repents."—LUKE 15:10 (NLT)

What if you were fighting a battle and you found out that heaven itself was on your side—or, rather, that you are on heaven's side?

Luke 15 describes God's love for the lost and how heaven rejoices when one is found. Heaven is waiting with streamers and balloons and confetti in hand.

There is a partnership with heaven wherever the Lord's invitation to agreement is sprinkled everywhere. Earthly happenings cause heaven itself to rejoice. Heaven is not merely busy with heavenly things but is very much connected to earthly participation. When Jesus taught us to pray, he included the phrase *"as it is in heaven."* And when the birth of Jesus was announced in Luke 2, the heavenly host declared "Glory to God in the highest, *and on earth* peace, good will toward men."

Agree with, *here*, what is celebrated *there*. Value here on earth the things that are valued in heaven.

It's as though He is peeling back a curtain to reveal the beauty of heavenly rejoicing as it relates to the great gospel news of Jesus bringing salvation to humankind here on earth. And He does so to strengthen our hearts!

Heaven itself is waiting for returned sinners.

Prayer

Father, I thank you for the uniqueness of the gospel and for its transforming power. I thank you that heaven itself rejoices in the return of our sons and daughters. Challenge our conventional, small expectations when it comes to your pursuit of and rejoicing over humankind. Amen.

Day Twelve

REHEARSE GOODNESS

I will remember the deeds of the LORD;
   yes, I will remember your wonders of old.
I will ponder all your work,
   and meditate on your mighty deeds.
Your way, O God, is holy.
   What god is great like our God?
You are the God who works wonders;
   you have made known your might among the peoples.
You with your arm redeemed your people,
   the children of Jacob and Joseph.—PSALM 77:11–15 (ESV)

I will tell of the kindnesses of the LORD,
   the deeds for which he is to be praised,
   according to all the LORD *has done for us—*
yes, the many good things
   he has done.—ISAIAH 63:7 (NIV)

Review His promises. Review your history with God.

When you remember His goodness your confidence in the Father increases. Remembering His goodness will cultivate trust. Remembering His goodness honors what He is doing and saying.

Rehearsing His goodness releases grace and quiet trust that bring stability.

Rehearse His goodness out loud. Thankful words spoken at the right time can make an eternal difference. Sometimes it's difficult to speak words of life, comfort, and encouragement when your heart is discouraged. Life-giving words are a game changer. There's something about words that changes the atmosphere of a situation.

What are you saying? What words are you speaking and confessing? Are your words consistent with His goodness? Do they nurture and build? Are they carefully shaped with gratitude?

Frame your words in the light of the truth of God's Word. Send an encouraging text today, filled with joy and gratitude and grace. It doesn't need to be long and profound. Write a simple note on a yellow-stickie note and put it on the bathroom mirror of your loved one.

Remind your own heart and remind others.

Prayer

Father, I thank you for your goodness! I rehearse your goodness and ask you to fill my mouth with words that bring life! Let me remember the wonders you have done and all the amazing things you have planned for us. I live with the expectancy that, knowing you were good in the past, you will be good in the future. It's who you are. Remembering your goodness fills me with faith this very day. Amen.

Day Thirteen

BEHOLD

Behold, God is my salvation,
I will trust and not be afraid;
"For YAH, the LORD, is my strength and song;
He also has become my salvation." —ISAIAH 12:2 (NKJV)

Depending on which translation you're using, there is no shortage of *beholds* in the Scriptures. Usually, the word means "sit up and pay attention!" Listen up.

Oftentimes, I pass over the word out of familiarity. I don't truly sit with it and actually "behold."

Prayer allows me to sit and behold. Forcing my heart to "sit down and pay attention" allows me to behold Him. Beholding Him changes me. It recalibrates my heart, my values, and my decisions. When I behold Him, I remember that He is truly with me. Beholding moves beyond impersonal promises and allows me to live in the experience of His abiding presence.

We are not changed by our efforts, but we are changed by the transformation work of beholding Him.

When we behold, we see wondrous things in His Word. When we cultivate awe and wonder, our hearts become soft and tender. Beholding Him allows us to resist the temptation to despair and give up.

Prayer

Father, I choose to sit and behold you today. I ask for the gift of spiritual sight and of seeing the beauty found in your Word and in your presence. I thank you for the gift of salvation. I will trust you and not be afraid. Amen.

Day Fourteen

THE LORD IS MY SHEPHERD

The LORD is my shepherd, I lack nothing.
He makes me lie down in green pastures,
he leads me beside quiet waters,
he refreshes my soul.
He guides me along the right paths
for his name's sake.
Even though I walk
through the darkest valley,
I will fear no evil,
for you are with me;
your rod and your staff,
they comfort me.

You prepare a table before me
in the presence of my enemies.
You anoint my head with oil;
my cup overflows.
Surely your goodness and love will follow me
all the days of my life,
and I will dwell in the house of the LORD
forever.—PSALM 23 (NIV)

There is unusual grace found in valleys. There is a measure of His presence found only in the lowlands.

Know that when you are walking through a valley you are most certainly not alone. The Shepherd is with you. He is ALL that you need. He IS your rest in green meadows, and He wants to lead you beside the peaceful streams of His presence.

He longs to renew your strength.

Our prodigal season produced an intimate understanding of the Shepherd heart of God. Since the 23rd psalm is so well known, there is the danger of its becoming stale in our hearts. Our season made way for us to connect with our good Shepherd in a deep way, allowing us to hear His voice in all its authority and credibility.

He is available to guide you, bringing honor to His own name. His beauty and love chase after you in both directions, covering all the days behind and all the ones in front of you. He lays you down in lush meadows and finds quiet pools for you to drink from. He is always, always true to His Word. His faithful rod and staff protect and comfort you and make you feel secure because, goodness knows, it can be hard to feel secure in a valley. Look around and see your cup overflowing with blessings.

See His goodness and mercy and unfailing love pursuing you.

Prayer

Father, I thank you for the unusual grace you have reserved for valleys. I thank you that you are walking with us in the bottom of this canyon. I thank you for the measure of your presence that is found uniquely in here. I receive it with quiet trust. Amen.

Day Fifteen

YOUR FAVORITE VERSE

Deep calls to deep
in the roar of your waterfalls;
all your waves and breakers
have swept over me.—Psalm 42:7 (NIV)

Each and every one of us has a favorite verse. A verse we can't shake. It's sticky. It sticks to us and holds us together. Usually, it's a particular word or a phrase that jumps off the page and straight into our spirits. I'm not about the tattoo'ed life, but if I were I would most certainly tattoo this psalm to my . . . see? I can't even finish that sentence with a straight face.

I'm a mountain girl. I live in the center of these United States, far from the ocean. I confess to having a fear/terror/healthy respect for all things oceanic. It makes no sense that this psalm, painted with words referring to deep waters, waterfalls, waves, and breakers, has attached itself to me.

Without minimizing my love for the entire 103rd Psalm, if I had to choose one verse that I cannot shake, it would be Psalm 42:7, for sure. I can't even begin to unpack the depth of mystery and beauty in this verse, which is probably why I can't shake it.

I prayed it over my prodigal son. I prayed that the deep things of God would call to the deep things of my son. I prayed that my son would respond to the deeper things of the Lord. I prayed that the Spirit of God would reach deeply into my son like a waterfall. I prayed that wave after wave of the Spirit would break over him. Over and over.

Pray your favorite verse over your loved one. The verse you can't shake.

Prayer

Father, I ask that my children would respond to the Spirit's deep calling. I pray that they would know a deeper relationship through the work of Jesus. I pray that they would know the depth of your greatness and the great things you have in mind for them. Amen.

Day Sixteen

NAME

But now, God's Message,
> *the God who made you in the first place, Jacob,*
> *the One who got you started, Israel:*
"Don't be afraid, I've redeemed you.
> *I've called your name. You're mine.*
When you're in over your head, I'll be there with you.
> *When you're in rough waters, you will not go down.*
When you're between a rock and a hard place,
> *it won't be a dead end—*
Because I am GOD, your personal God,
> *The Holy of Israel, your Savior.*
I paid a huge price for you:
> *all of Egypt, with rich Cush and Seba thrown in!*
That's how much you mean to me!
> *That's how much I love you!*
I'd sell of the whole world to get you back,
> *trade the creation just for you."*—ISAIAH 43:1–4 (MSG)

It goes without saying that our choice in baby names goes way beyond "What name goes well with our last name?" Like all other parents-to-be, we poured over baby name books to find a name that seemed to fit each one of our children. A name that carried the weight of blessing. A name with destiny. A name that would describe the boundary lines of their journey.

When we were expecting our fifth child, as we suspected a "she" would be born after a steady stream of boys, we found a trendy name that "sounded" good with our last name, but meant "barren." I just couldn't.

Pray over the name you chose for your child. Redeem that name.

For example, we named our third child "Levi," and his name means "joined, attached" in Hebrew. In the Bible Levi was in the priestly tribe of Israel, like Moses and Aaron, and our prayers for our own Levi are often that he would continue to be "joined and attached" to the Lord. Every time I read a priestly verse in the Bible, I pray for our son Levi.

Levi is now twenty-two years old. He is joined and attached to the Lord. He is thriving in graduate school and leading a small group through the local church he attends. He ministers to others with complete ease and a lack of striving. It just flows from him.

Pray over the name you chose for your child. Redeem that name.

Prayer

Father, I thank you that you've called us each by name. You've called us your own. You are not just for us but you are with us. I pray for our child and the good things you have in mind. I thank you that you paid the ultimate price for our child. Amen.

Day Seventeen

PRAY CORPORATELY

Peter was kept in prison, but the church was earnestly praying to God for him.

The night before Herod was to bring him to trial, Peter was sleeping between two soldiers, bound with two chains, and sentries stood guard at the entrance. Suddenly an angel of the Lord appeared and a light shone in the cell. He struck Peter on the side and woke him up. "Quick, get up!" he said, and the chains fell off Peter's wrists.

Then the angel said to him, "Put on your clothes and sandals." And Peter did so. "Wrap your cloak around you and follow me," the angel told him. Peter followed him out of the prison, but he had no idea that what the angel was doing was really happening; he thought he was seeing a vision. They passed the first and second guards and came to the iron gate leading to the city.—ACTS 12:5–10 (NIV)

When I was a little girl, I always checked Acts 12 when I saw a Bible sitting on a coffee table, in a pew back, or on a Sunday school shelf. Obviously, I was curious to see if my name was in every copy, or just in the copies we had at home.

Now I have a different love for Acts 12. I love how Peter's imprisonment ignited a constant prayer force offered to God from the church. I love how the angel told him to gird himself and tie his sandals. I love how Rhoda and her prayer meeting friends were astonished that their prayers were actually answered.

The church prayed and Peter was freed.

Praying alone for our personal need is a lifeline, but in Matthew 18:19–20 God describes the unique power of two or three gathering in His name to pray. Some answers to prayer are waiting for a corporate participation and gathering of faith. There are aspects to prayer that can only be complete when we join with other believers.

Prayer meetings are a funny thing because Jesus' representatives are sometimes flawed, and those meetings can get messy. Jesus himself has no flaws or failures. No defects. Somehow, those in the early church, in all their flawed humanity, "devoted themselves to prayer." I'm sure it was a glorious mess.

I would love to start a worldwide prayer movement devoted to calling prodigals home. Until that day, grab the hands of two or three faithful (messy) friends and pray. Read Acts 12 again if you need a reminder of the transforming power of prayer.

Involve others in this prayer journey.

Prayer

Father, You desire to set captives free. We pray that you would break chains over our sons and daughters. We come against addiction in the authority of your name. We pray for freedom according to your will. Amen.

Day Eighteen

THE ONE WHO SEES ME

*The angel of the LORD found Hagar near a spring in the desert;
it was the spring that is beside the road to Shur. And he said,
"Hagar, slave of Sarai, where have you come from, and where
are you going?"*

"I'm running away from my mistress Sarai," she answered.

Then the angel of the LORD told her, "Go back to your mistress and submit to her." The angel added, "I will increase your descendants so much that they will be too numerous to count."

The angel of the LORD also said to her:

"You are now pregnant
    and you will give birth to a son.
You shall name him Ishmael,
    for the LORD has heard of your misery.
He will be a wild donkey of a man;
    his hand will be against everyone
    and everyone's hand against him,
and he will live in hostility
    toward all his brothers."

*She gave this name to the LORD who spoke to her: "You are
the God who sees me," for she said, "I have now seen the One who
sees me."*—GENESIS 16:7–13 (NIV)

Sometimes it's easier to believe in God's greatness on a grand scale—in His creating the heavens and the earth, the cosmos, the ocean tides and the majestic landscapes—than it is to believe in his ability to see (or care about) our personal pain.

When Hagar found herself in a miserable slave girl situation, partly due to her own actions, her station, and the harsh treatment of others, she encountered the God of the cosmos, who saw her. Watched over her. With plans to bless her wild donkey of a son. In spaces of desolation and despair. She met Jehovah El Roi, The God Who Sees Me.

She didn't just *feel* abandoned, she *was* abandoned. She had no place.

Her story continues in chapter 21, where she placed her son under a bush in the desert of Beersheba, looking away, as she expected to die without water. And once again God intervened. He heard the boy crying and sent an angel to rescue them and reveal a water well.

God sees. He knows. He longs to reveal Himself to you with great compassion and providence. He longs to reveal His plan for you.

He is the God who sees you.

Prayer

Father, I praise you for seeing the whole story. You see it all, from beginning to end. I confess that my vision of the present is clouded and that I can't even begin to see how good will come of our present situation. I feel alone and abandoned, but I choose to trust your watchful care. Increase my awareness of your watchful presence. Amen.

Day Nineteen

ABIDE

"I am the vine; you are the branches. Whoever abides in me and I in him, he it is that bears much fruit, for apart from me, you can do nothing."—John 15:5 (ESV)

In seasons of disappointment, it's tempting to lean into the Lord for an immediate "situational rescue," but if we're not careful we might miss the deeper rescue of our souls, which is found as we depend completely on Him.

These seasons can often unearth and expose our independent heart conditions. Buried under seasons of ease, rivers of self-righteousness flow unchallenged. When faced with structural collapse, we mercifully come to know that apart from the vine-dresser we can do nothing.

In my fifty-one years, I have come to understand that I can keep humans alive, but not plants. Recently, in a great move of faith, I purchased three Costco houseplants with steely determination that I would keep them alive. I. Will. Keep. Them. Alive.

While I have no green thumb, I am growing in understanding the basic principles of pruning and trimming and watering—or in my case, severe over-watering.

While waiting for my prodigal child, I was pruned back for greater strength. I was watered—not too much, but in just the right amounts. I was fertilized, but the properties of the compost felt filthy and stinky. The pruning felt brutal and left me unrecognizable, but when the season gave way to fruit I recognized greater usefulness and purpose. The water came in just the right doses. The fertilizer added insult to injury, but my branches emerged stronger and my roots deeper.

Allowing His work in my life through the brutal season gave way to a deeper abiding.

I came to a greater understanding of His nature as a Gardener, and I released my death grip of independence and self-sufficiency. I discovered great rescue, not from my situation, but the soul rescue that comes with daily abiding.

Prayer

Father, I trust you as the Gardener who prunes back branches for greater strength and usefulness and fruitfulness. Increase my dependence on you in all things. As I abide in you, help me to move beyond self-sufficiency to the full range of potential found in you alone. As I move away from self-sufficiency, demonstrate greater compassion in and through me. Amen.

Day Twenty

PRAY HONESTLY

And they went to a place called Gethsemane. And [Jesus] said to his disciples, "Sit here while I pray." And he took with him Peter and James and John along with him, and he began to be deeply distressed and troubled. "My soul is overwhelmed with sorrow to the point of death," he said to them. "Stay here and keep watch." Going a little farther, he fell to the ground and prayed that if possible the hour might pass from him. "Abba, Father," he said, "everything is possible for you. Take this cup from me. Yet not what I will, but what you will."—MARK 14:32–36 (ESV)

I often put this passage from Mark 14 in a *to-be-opened-during-Easter-season-only* box, in the same way Luke 2 feels like an *open-in-December* box. When I allow my ears to listen to the words of Jesus outside the Easter season, however, I find this prayer to be an invitation to honestly lament before the Lord.

Jesus was praying for a way out. God's very own Son, who knew what He had come to earth for, felt the full weight of anguish and asked for a few faithful friends to come and sit with Him while he poured out His distress to the Father.

These images are no small thing. Jesus, our own Jesus, was deeply distressed and troubled. He described His own soul as overwhelmed with sorrow to the point of death. He fell to the ground in anguish.

Jesus is giving us permission to fall on our faces and grieve our disappointment. He gave us permission to pray with honesty. Praying honestly doesn't necessarily mean that we don't trust the Lord. He models a posture of honest, gut-wrenching prayer that can be poured out to the Father without fear of His accusation.

After expressing His lament, He turned His heart upward, like the psalmist, and confessed that "everything is possible for you. Take this cup from me. Yet not what I will, but what you will." He began with gut-wrenching, honest lament and ended with a beautiful surrender to the Father's will.

Your agony and anguish don't need to be polished before they can be brought to the Lord. Bring them. Honestly. And when you've expressed your heart-rending, honest lament, surrender. Open your weary hands and remember that everything is possible for Him.

Father, I pour my soul out to you and trust that you will hear my cry. I'm deeply distressed and troubled, and I bring it to you. Everything is possible for you. Not what I attempt to maneuver or manipulate, but *your will* be done. Forgive me for the fear that I've allowed to settle around my heart. Help me reclaim the wonder and vision you have in mind for us. Again, your will be done. Amen.

Day Twenty-One

JESUS IS OUR HOPE

*For God so loved the world that he gave his one and only Son,
that whoever believes in him shall not perish but have eternal
life. For God did not send his Son into the world to condemn the
world, but to save the world through him. Whoever believes in
him is not condemned, but whoever does not believe stands condemned already because they have not believed in the name of
God's one and only Son.*—JOHN 3:16–18 (NIV)

Take a moment and reflect on the One to whom we have been pointing our hearts for the past twenty days. Our downcast eyes are now
lifted to Jesus. Our hopeless hearts are encouraged by Jesus. We've
been pushing back against the pressure of hopelessness through
the reality of Jesus.

Jesus is the hope of the earth and the hope for our prodigal sons
and daughters.

At the intersection of excruciating heartache and beautiful, joyous grace, I invite you to discover and rediscover the hope found in
Jesus alone. In contrast to the ugly underbelly of disappointment,
lift your gaze by the beauty of His daily presence. The answer to
the pain and seemingly grave injustices of this life is found in Jesus
alone. In the midst of every broken situation and sorrow there is
certain hope.

Our hope is not based on our ability to muster up sufficient strength and power through our own great determination and positivity. Our hope is not about pixie-dusted wishful thinking and blind optimism, *even though I shall always love pinning myself a good old pair of bedazzled Tink wings on tiny shoulders.* Our hope rests in Jesus alone— and He is enough. Our hope rests in the One who offers hope for all our brokenhearted, disappointed, and weary moments.

The hope of Jesus brings life and joy and rest and peace for this beautiful, broken life.

For those who long to see a prodigal son or daughter return, rest your hope in Jesus.

Prayer

Father, you are with me in hopeful expectation. I thank you for stepping down from heaven through your Son, Jesus. I fully trust you with the future of my prodigal child. I set my hope in Jesus alone. Amen.

SECTION THREE

Family Recipes

Family Recipes

All at once an angel touched him and said, "Get up and eat."
[Elijah] looked around, and there by his head was some bread
baked over hot coals, and a jar of water. He ate and drank and
then lay down again.

The angel of the LORD came back a second time and touched
him and said, "Get up and eat, for the journey is too much for
you." So he got up and ate and drank. Strengthened by that food,
he traveled forty days and forty nights until he reached Horeb,
the mountain of God.—1 KINGS 19:5–8 (NIV)

Because of the way I'm hardwired, family recipes played a major role throughout our prodigal story. Without trying to over-spiritualize the role food might play in the gathering of families, I'll point out that in the above section the Lord seems to be interested in Elijah's emotional, spiritual, psychological, *and* physical well-being. Before telling the distraught Elijah to get up, he takes the time to feed him.

At the very least, Scripture often points to God's working through tables and feasts and banquets. The early church enjoyed many things, including the gathering together for meals with glad and sincere hearts. Revelation tells us that our future in heaven includes the marriage supper of the Lamb.

As I waited for my prodigal child to return, preparing homemade food was my way of loving him, serving him, reminding him, and strengthening him. It was often the best language I could speak.

I've often said that my faith was formed in the kitchens of my grandmothers, and my children's faith was formed in my own. For one child, his faith was lost. And found. For this I will forever be praising God. On his journey home, one of the ways I loved him was by baking *some bread over hot coals.*

Sounds like a tortilla to me.

Rhoda's Brisket Tacos

I've tried preparing my brisket dried and rubbed, fat-side up, fat-side down, on a rack, on a bed of onions, and wrapped in foil—I've tried it all. I promise this is the best way to prepare brisket tacos. Dump all the ingredients in a crockpot and go to bed. Sleep like a baby while visions of brisket tacos dance in your head.

....

Place brisket in a slow cooker. Mix all ingredients and pour it over the brisket. Cover with lid and cook on LOW for 10 hours (overnight).

Serve brisket inside warm corn tortillas and top with fresh pico de gallo.

Sing glory.

* La Costeña or Embasa brand chipotle peppers can be found in the "Hispanic/International Food" aisle of your local grocery store. Look for the bottles of pace picante sauce or Old El Paso taco shells, and you'll know you're in the right place!

Ingredients

3 tablespoons vegetable oil

5 garlic cloves, peeled

1 teaspoon paprika

2 teaspoons salt

1½ teaspoons garlic powder

1¼ teaspoons black pepper

1½ teaspoons onion powder

½ teaspoon dried oregano

½ teaspoon dried thyme

2 cans beef broth

1 cup ketchup

1 can chipotle peppers in adobo sauce*

1 cup light brown sugar

8-10 pound brisket

Notes

_____

_____

_____

_____

_____

Rosalie's Breakfast Burritos

My mama's name is Rosalie, and she is 100 pounds soaking wet of pure, solid gold. She believes that flip-flops are the third most dangerous shoe, which has nothing to do with her breakfast burritos but gives you a small taste of the joy that is my mother.

The key to her breakfast burritos are the fresh grated russet potatoes, fried in oil with a dash of salt and pepper. It's the simple things. She used to grate her potatoes with a good old-fashioned box cheese grater, and now she shreds those bad boys with her trusty Cuisinart food processor in record time.

Ingredients

vegetable oil

8 ounces fresh Mexican-style chorizo, casings removed

4 large russet potatoes, grated

8 large eggs

salt and pepper

tortillas

½ cup finely shredded cheddar cheese

Heat 2 tablespoons vegetable oil in large skillet over medium-high heat. Add chorizo and cook, breaking it up with a wooden spoon until crisp, about 5 minutes. Remove to a paper-towel-lined plate using a slotted spoon.

With paper towel, wipe the skillet and add an additional 2 tablespoons vegetable oil. Add the grated potatoes and fry, stirring occasionally, until the potatoes are golden brown and crisp, for 8–10 minutes. Set aside.

Scramble eggs. Set aside.

One at a time, warm the tortillas on a griddle or skillet (comal) and build the burrito by layering the scrambled eggs, fried potatoes, and chorizo. Finish with a sprinkle of cheese before rolling.

Bless God.

Grandma Rose's Spanish Rice

My grandma began dinner prep the moment her breakfast dishes were cleared. Roasts would be bound, roasted chile peeled, and pinto beans would be cleaned and soaking by 10 a.m.

Her fideo, rice, or fried potatoes were the final touch on any and every dinner. She would toss a handful of frozen peas into her rice, but my family is not crazy about peas, so I add chopped celery hearts.

Ingredients

2 cups long grain rice

3 cups chicken broth

1 can Rotel® tomatoes

celery hearts/frozen peas

pinch of cumin

....

In a heavy pan, toast rice in oil over medium high heat. Stir constantly. After rice looks brown, add a handful of chopped celery hearts (or frozen peas) and a pinch of cumin and continue to stir for a minute.

Pour chicken broth and Rotel over the hot toasted rice and stir until boiling. Cover and turn the heat to low and simmer for 25 minutes.

Sing praises to the Lamb.

Notes

_____

_____

_____

_____

_____

Torrez Family Homemade Tortillas

My grandmother's rolling pin was an actual extension of her right hand. I'm telling you, it moved with ninja speed. She also played the tambourine with her rolling hand during worship as she sang coritos at the top of her lungs. I'm a mere shadow of her greatness.

Back to her rolling pin.

It was the size of a medium dowel rod, or broom handle, and she rolled perfectly round tortillas with one hand while flipping the cooked ones with her Teflon-tough left hand.

Combine dry ingredients in medium sized bowl and add lard. Add water, slowly, and work mixture into a dough. Knead dough until smooth, cover, and set aside for 10 minutes.

Divide the dough into equal pieces, each about the size of a golf ball. Roll each ball of dough into a 6-inch circle.

Heat griddle or skillet (comal) on medium-high heat. Place each tortilla on griddle and cook for 1 minute on each side until light brown speckles blister through the dough.

Gloria a Dios!

Notes

_____

_____

_____

_____

Rosalie's Biscochitos

According to my mama, the key to biscochitos is dry-toasting the anise seeds in a pan before crushing them. I don't argue—I simply obey.

Heat a small skillet over medium heat. Once hot, add the anise seeds and stir gently. Keep the seeds moving in the pan for about a minute or until they begin to smell ah-mazing and toasty. After toasting the seeds, place them in a sandwich baggie and crush them with a rolling pin. Genius.

....

Preheat oven to 350°.

Sift flour with baking powder and salt. In a separate bowl, cream lard with sugar and toasted anise seeds until fluffy. Beat in egg. On low speed, add orange juice and flour mixture to lard mixture.

Turn dough out on a lightly floured board and roll to ¼ inch thickness. Cut into shapes and toss in cinnamon and sugar before laying them on the cookie sheet. Bake for 13 minutes until bottoms of cookie are slightly brown.

Merry Christmas, ya filthy animal.

Ingredients

3 cups all-purpose flour

1 ½ teaspoons baking powder

¼ teaspoon salt

1 cup Snow Cap® lard, room temperature

¾ cup granulated sugar

1 large egg, room temperature

1½ teaspoons ground and toasted anise seeds

½ cup orange juice

¼ cup granulated sugar + 1 tablespoon ground cinnamon for topping

Notes

Rhoda's Baked Oatmeal

This recipe is adapted from a recipe I was introduced to as a "football mom" back in the day. Over the years I adjusted it to my family's taste, eliminated the extra brown sugar topping, because—Good Lord!—it has enough sugar, and added almond extract, because any chance to use almond extract makes me happy.

Also, brace yourself for the amount of butter. Really, brace yourself.

Ingredients

6 cups oats

3 ½ cups milk

2½ cups brown sugar

3½ sticks butter (gulp)

4 extra large eggs

2 tablespoons baking powder

1 teaspoon salt

1 teaspoon almond extract

Spray 9x13 baking pan with Pam spray and add oats and milk. Stir together in the pan and let sit while mixing the other ingredients.

Cream together brown sugar and butter. To the sugar/butter mixture, add eggs, baking powder, salt, and almond extract. Mix well.

Stir into oat/milk mixture and mix well.

Bake @ 325° for 35 minutes. The kids like it slightly runny in the middle and a little more baked around the edges. Serve warm.

Praise Him!

Notes

_____

_____

_____

_____

_____

Mrs. Schultz's Hot German Potato Salad

(Warmer Kartoffelsalat)

My husband's memories of his childhood dinners were meals I'd never heard of before. Dishes like *salmon loaf* and *chipped beef on toast*. He didn't even know what a burrito was until he saw a little brown girl named Linda Vigil unwrap her foiled lunch in the fifth grade.

In the same vein, I had never once seen a *bratwurst* or *hot German potato salad* in my years. But it was love at first creamy, tangy, bacon-dripped bite.

Ingredients

2 pounds red potatoes

salt

½ cup diced bacon

½ cup onion

1½ teaspoons flour

4 teaspoons sugar

dash of pepper

¼ to ⅓ cup vinegar

½ cup water

2 tablespoons Italian parsley

Cook potatoes until fork tender, then cut into slices. In small skillet, fry bacon until crisp. Add onion and sauté until just tender, not brown.

Meanwhile, in a bowl, mix flour, sugar, salt, and pepper. Stir in vinegar (amount depends on tartness desired) and water until smooth. Add to bacon, then simmer until slightly thickened. Pour this hot dressing over potatoes. Yum.

Garnish with Italian parsley and serve hot.

Gott ist gut!

Notes